Making Living Lovely

Russell Whitehead Jordan Cluroe

Making Living Lovely

Free Your Home with Creative Design

with over 250 illustrations

Thames & Hudson

A DEDICATION

Thank you to our mums for allowing us to
decorate our childhood bedrooms with them. Thank you
to the wonderful online community of interior lovers.
Your support and your work keep us constantly fuelled and
excited about design. And to our beloved Buckley, the wonder
dog, who is always there to make us feel better when we hit
difficult times and to keep our feet on the ground
when we have the good times.

On the back cover: Jordan (left) and Russell (right).
Page 1: The bathroom at Hither Green (see page 43).
Page 2: The living room at Perry Rise (see page 195).
Pages 3–4: 2LG's first project on Cloudesley Road in London.

First published in the United Kingdom in 2020 by
Thames & Hudson Ltd, 181A High Holborn,
London WC1V 7QX

Making Living Lovely: Free Your Home with Creative Design
© 2020 Thames & Hudson Ltd, London
Text © 2020 2LG Studio
Photography © 2020 Megan Taylor
For all other illustrations, please see the picture
credits list on page 206.

Designed by Therese Vandling

British Library Cataloguing-in-Publication Data
A catalogue record for this book is available
from the British Library

ISBN 978-0-500-02269-6

Printed and bound in China by 1010 Printing International Ltd

To find out about all our publications, please visit
www.thamesandhudson.com. There you can subscribe to
our e-newsletter, browse or download our current catalogue,
and buy any titles that are in print.

Contents

Introduction

This is a book about empowerment, identity, kindness and pride. It is about understanding who you live with and the way you want to live. It is about helping you to make a home that facilitates your life and lifts your spirits.

If you are feeling overwhelmed, stuck in a rut, nervous about where to start with your interior, out of inspiration or overloaded with it, this book can help. Our approach isn't about following strict 'design rules'. Instead, we want to give you the tools to create a lovely home that both is inspired by you and inspires you every day.

It is our firm belief that whether your home is rented or owned, temporary or long term, you deserve to live in a wonderful space. In return, your space deserves respect and to be given the freedom to fulfil its potential. No matter how modest or grand the design vision for your home, the process of realizing it comes back to the same things: bravery, openness and giving yourself the freedom to create. Read on to find out how design can change your life in simple ways. You have the power to make it happen.

Who Are 2LG?

We are Jordan and Russell – or the 2 Lovely Gays, as we are fondly known – a married couple and interior design duo who live and work together in South London with our mini dachshund, Buckley the wonder dog.

Since launching our design practice, 2LG Studio, we have travelled the world designing homes for our clients, creating new products, seeking out great design and exploring the way we live in our homes today.

We've rented, we've owned and we've worked with budgets big and small. Together, we've lived in, and decorated, several homes, and our current passion project, the Design House, is a complete renovation that we use to showcase our style and design ideas via our social media channels.

Our background is in theatre and television and we worked successfully as actors for nearly a decade. Soon after we met, we started visiting museums and festivals around the world together and created our first home, unlocking a shared passion for design in the process. We started out screenprinting our textile designs; then, over time, our love of design grew and eventually overtook acting as our first love. When you have applied yourself at a high level in any creative field, you learn valuable lessons about what it takes to deliver a creative idea. As interior designers, we still work as creatives in much the same way we did as actors, just using slightly different tools.

Eventually we dived into our own interior design business and worked on some amazing projects, from boutique hotels to head offices and celebrity homes, and we haven't looked back since. Our design work has been featured all over the world, in top magazines and on online platforms, and we have also collaborated with globally renowned design brands in London, Paris and New York. Together we want nothing short of an interiors revolution – placing importance on wonderful design and decorative joy in equal measure to help make living lovely.

#makinglivinglovely

Lovely is a reaction against shame, fear and hate. We want you to live in a lovely world, not a cruel one. We want kindness to be the key and we made a choice a long time ago to be positive in our approach to interior design. This is challenging sometimes, especially when life is getting you down.

When we started our interiors business, some people in the industry told us the word 'lovely' was too soft – not mysterious, not 'design'. This only spurred us on to break down those barriers. We had no idea we would be starting something that is about so much more than just redesigning rooms.

Lovely is everything that makes you who you are and who you want to be. Lovely is kind, but it can also be excellent. Our approach to design is a holistic one and our hope is to make you feel supported and confident in making your own choices and executing your creativity in your own time. No pressure, just happy homes. We feel very grateful to have the opportunity and a platform to share our voice with you.

Designers on Home

Different approaches are equally valid and nowhere more so than in the home. Since starting our practice, we have discovered a strong international community of inspirational fellow designers and have interviewed ten of them specially for this book. Throughout this book, you will find their individual insights into what home means to them, offering a range of perspectives on interior design, lighting, ceramics, print and products, always with creativity as the focus. We've even asked them what movie their home would be, to give you a completely different reference point.

Our Design House

Alongside the features on our interior design projects for lovely clients that you will find throughout this book, we want to share with you the experience of fully modernizing our dilapidated Victorian house, Perry Rise. Working on the project for the past five years has helped us craft a new creative approach to interiors. Each design element in our home has a story and we will share some of these with you in this book to explore the different routes an interior design can take.

The process of designing our home has presented unexpected opportunities and revealed new styles. Personal style is frequently discussed in the media, but the truth is that your unique style is influenced by the experiences in your life and can only evolve with time. We hope sharing our home story will give you the confidence to take on your own project.

Introduction

Design is Not a Luxury, it's a Lifestyle

Interiors are important. From waiting rooms to high-end dining experiences, the rooms we spend time in play key roles in our society and impact our experiences, the way we feel and even our health. The same is true of your home. If you are going to fulfil your potential, you need a home that facilitates this – a space filled with the wonder of you.

Interior design is not just about cushions, as architecture is not just about bricks. The colours you see, the objects you surround yourself with and the flooring you feel underfoot have everything to do with your life and the way you live it. So, while we don't take ourselves too seriously, we take design very seriously. Interiors matter and getting them right can make your life better.

We get asked about property value all the time. 'Will I decrease my house price if I create a bold interior?' The only way you can damage the value of your home is with bad workmanship or a confused design. Clarity of vision, beautifully carried out, will always be an asset, and working with what you have and learning to buy right will help you achieve this. We are not here to make you change everything you own and buy all-new to create a 'look'. Far from it. We want you to invest time in yourself and take a moment to consider what works and what doesn't, so you can find your own way.

Live in your home for the now, not for the day you sell. A home is not about perfection, the finish line and the big reveal, it is about growth. There will be hurdles – or 'wobbles' as we call them – along the way while you piece together your interior scheme, but these are part of your home's journey. We want to inspire you to take your style to an unexpected place and give you the confidence to make informed decisions about your home and how you want to live in it.

<u>BELOW</u>

An illustration by Joe Gamble of us and Buckley the wonder dog at work in the design studio.

Introduction

A Note on Kindness

What you put out comes back to you – it's a basic law of the universe. If you put positivity and love into your home, it will come back to you in your life, so on your journey to self-discovery through design, be kind to others (and to animals, for that matter), but also – and perhaps most importantly – <u>be kind to yourself</u>.

Stop judging yourself, stop worrying what anyone else thinks, and look after your own needs for a bit. When you take care of yourself by creating a home that nurtures your soul, refuels your human solar panels and facilitates your dreams, you will be much better equipped to be kind to the rest of the world.

Remember to have your own back and banish shame. Your home may not be where you want it to be just yet, but all the best homes evolve. Trust us, you will get there. You have already taken the first step to getting your home on track by picking up this book.

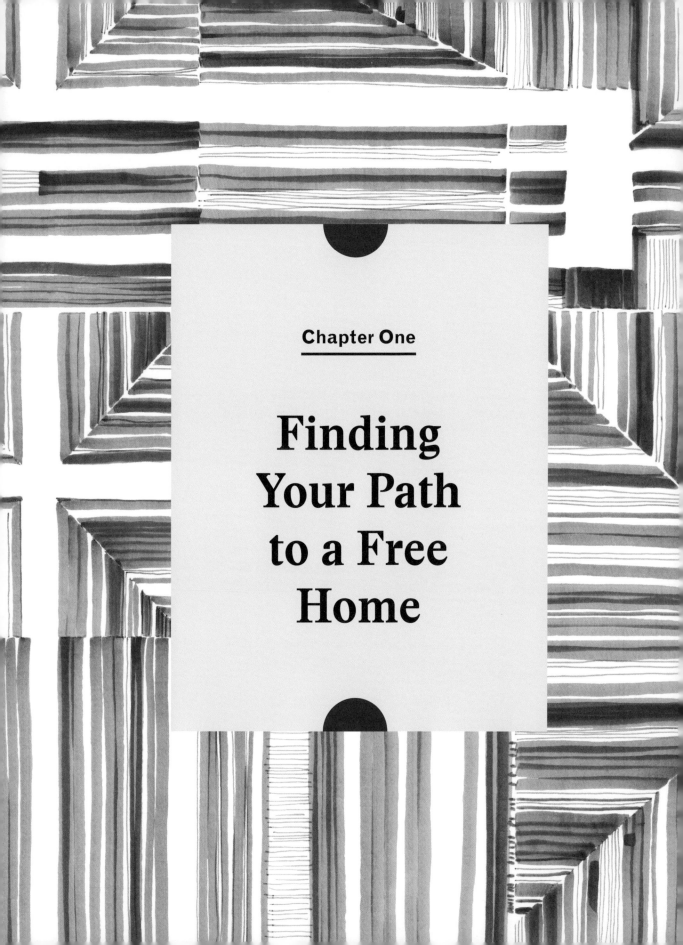

Chapter One

Finding Your Path to a Free Home

The challenges we face in our homes are universal, international and multi-generational, from sustainability, well-being and a lack of space to inspiration overload and a daily bombardment of images via social media. It can all get too much.

Our living spaces should express our personalities and facilitate our needs, but they often end up as a source of embarrassment and shame. The home you live in says so much about you and of course you want to represent yourself in the right way. The pressure is real and can lead to a reluctance to commit to ideas and get in the way of creating a home that's true to you.

Put down that paintbrush for a moment and breathe. In this chapter, we explore the obstacles you may be facing on your path to interior design confidence and help you to move forward without judgment. The only person you need to keep up with is yourself, so free yourself from criticism. If you focus on expressing your story, what other people think will cease to matter. This can apply to other aspects of your life, of course, but your interior is a good place to start.

Free Yourself from Interiors FOMO

FOMO = Fear Of Missing Out
*creates negativity, a 'fug', a fuzziness, a green-eyed monster,
often aroused by posts seen on social media

We are in an age of massive cultural sharing. The uploading and consuming of ideas on Instagram, Pinterest, Facebook and the wider web have created an endlessly exciting visual mashup, bombarding us with all of human experience in a series of beautifully curated images that can enlighten and inspire, but more often paralyse us with indecision.

Fear of making the wrong impression can lock down your creative freedom without you even realizing. We've all been there. You've just redecorated your living room or renovated your house and suddenly the colour of the year changes, or you see an image on Insta that screams 'you', or your favourite designer brings out a new lighting range and you simply must have it and now you hate everything you own because you want the newest or coolest update. It's enough to make you lose sleep.

With so many ideas and the intense pressure to 'get it right', the struggle to find clarity is real. If this sounds like you, simply recognizing that you feel this way is a powerful first step. FOMO can do one!

Comparison is the Death of Creativity

Have you ever found yourself saying 'I was going to do that but someone else has already done it' or 'I want to give this a try, but I could never do it as well as that other person did'? If you keep constantly measuring yourself against what other people are doing, you will kill your creative journey before you've even started.

Other people's ideas must never stop you from doing you. We love social media as much as anyone, but external inspiration can only go so far when designing an interior.

First, clear your head and ask yourself these simple questions: How do I want to live? What do I need around me? What gives me decorative joy?

These may seem ridiculously obvious things to think about before you design your home, but they are often ignored. This book won't give you all the answers – you need to find those for yourself – but we do want to invest you with an inquisitive approach and the ability to know your own mind.

How do I want
to live?

What do I need
around me?

What gives me
decorative joy?

The End of Trend

'Trends can be useful to keep afloat in a sea of newness, but they must never steer the ship'

The Internet has made us more design savvy than ever and trends are becoming increasingly defunct as culture moves ever faster and in more directions. It's no longer straightforward for brands to just spoonfeed us ideas that maximize their sales. Authenticity is now key and our values are becoming the defining factor in our decision making. If you take the time to get to know your core values, you will find that trends roll off you without distracting you from your vision for your home, leaving you better able to express yourself in your interior.

A Note on Moodboarding

The first thing you might think of when starting an interior project is to create a moodboard. If you choose to moodboard, it can be incredibly fun and a rewarding part of your design process, but try to hold off until we get to materials, colour and pattern later in the book. If you are not sure about moodboards, what they are and how they can help, that's also fine. Too often a moodboard is slavishly forced into existence and set in stone, rather than coming to life naturally. To start with, we want you to focus on understanding and communicating your needs and those of the people you live with. Forget moodboards for now and think of this first stage as creating your 'storyboard' instead.

Chapter One

That Perfect Instagram Shot

So much of the interior design inspiration out there is instant gratification, a moment of wow for your eyes, but then it only serves to crush your own creativity. We want you to be able to reframe the images you pin and adore into something you can live with for you.

The truth is, in most of the lusted-after shots you see online and in print, the room outside the camera frame was probably in a total mess, full of stacked furniture and real-life clutter and, if you look hard at that mirror in the middle, you'll spot the reflection of the person behind the camera crouching with a coat over their head so your eye isn't drawn to them. The reality of creating the perfect image is placing chairs at bizarre angles to look good on camera and using more props than a Royal Shakespeare Company warehouse sale. You can't live in that shot. Don't get us wrong – we have been guilty of having the odd plug socket retouched and we love an aspirational image as much as the next person, but it's important is to see it for what it is.

You'll find no 'interiors porn' in this book because images can be part of the problem. If you aren't careful, they weigh you down, setting impossible challenges until you can't remember what you like – or even if you like anything at all. Trust us, we've been there. The images presented here each illustrate a point to help you along the way but we want you to look inside yourself first and foremost to enable you to take inspiration from the images you see and not be drowned by them. Understand 'interiors porn' and use it wisely.

Recognizing Your Inner Nemesis

Our approach to interiors is all about taking the time to understand the 'why'. Work out 'why' you want to change your home and the 'how' of getting it done will be so much easier. In order get to the all-important 'why', you first need to identify 'what' the problems are in your space.

It's now time to get to know yourself better and ask what is holding you back from taking your interior to the next level. This section is about recognizing patterns of behaviour that have not been working for you and making changes that will take you one step closer to finding your inner designer.

Over the years, we have come to notice three common personality traits in our clients and we want to bring them to your attention, not to embarrass you – that is so not our style – but to let you know that you are not alone. The hidden issues that are stopping your home from reaching its full potential are universal and once you recognize them, you can get on with creating a home that brings out the best version of yourself. If you have any of these character traits, or maybe even all three, that's fine. In fact, it's a good thing. There is no shame in seeing your weaknesses for what they are and owning them so you can better follow through with your designs.

The Home Shy

'I love it, but what if no one else does?' *(Quickly hides it away in a cupboard)*

Do you stop yourself from choosing that paint colour or fabric that makes your heart leap and opt for a palette that others will find more palatable? Do you have things you hide away when people come over to visit, such as silly knick-knacks that only you will understand or a favourite blanket that's a little raggedy? Do you have stacks of paintings and photos just waiting to be framed and hung, but you can't decide where to put them? Are all your walls white or cream? Still living with that sofa that's broken, as you haven't seen 'the one' yet? Do you have a secret stash of memorabilia or a 'room of doom' where you put anything that would give away your personality for fear of being judged? If you have things you love but haven't found a home for them then maybe you are 'home shy'.

The Inspiration Hoarder

'I love it, in fact, I love it all. Oh wait, I love that too!'

Are you an inspiration hoarder? We used to keep scrapbooks and magazine tear-outs, but now inspiration hoarding has moved online and ramped up a level with Pinterest, Instagram and likes, shares and saves galore. Do you have a back catalogue of 6,000 images somewhere that are all super inspiring, but it stops there and they never make it into your real life? Are you struggling to see what it is you love about an image? Is it the floors or is it just a feeling? You are overflowing with so much inspiration you may scream a little bit. It's overwhelming – and if this sounds like you, then we can help!

The Micro-Shopper

'I have to have this. I have no idea where to put it, but I simply must have it!'

Are you a micro-shopper – a magpie distracted by pretty, sparkly things? Are you constantly on the lookout for the next bargain, quick fix or latest fashion? The micro-shopper buys without thinking and is often sold on trends – from flamingos to pineapples and cacti, whatever the next big thing is, you want in. Easily attracted by new colours and shapes, you make purchases without planning where they will go. If you have made an impulse purchase recently and it still hasn't found a place in your home, or if you've ended up redesigning a whole room based on one new purchase, this is you.

TheOver-whelmed Space

Is your home bursting at the seams with stuff that you love, but can't live with? Have your interiors become over-the-top and overwhelming, with a clash of tastes and design decisions? Has the functionality of your everyday life become compromised by the constraints of your space and the stuff within it?

'The overwhelmed space' is a regular occurrence, in our experience. This is a space that is suffocated under the weight of multiple ideas and still houses all the stuff purchased by different versions of you from years gone by. It is filled with micro purchases and creative gambles that were so bold in their lack of thought that the space just can't cope. This home is no fun to live in.

The
Non-
Space

Or perhaps you are totally underwhelmed by your interior?
In trying not to be judged or make mistakes, have you become
trapped in a space that says nothing and makes you feel bored
or sad? Frozen by your indecision (or that of those around you),
you are stuck so fast in a rut that your space isn't anything.
You have ended up living with nothing nice around you and
no statement of who you are or what you need.

   We often see homes that feel cold and unloved because the
person who lives there is afraid to be judged for the choices
they make and therefore chooses to make no choices at all.
This results in 'the non-space' – a white box, a soulless home.
It doesn't need to be this way.

   If you recognize yourself in this, then you can begin to
address the issue and work on building the confidence to make
your home better.

Free Your Mind and Your Space Will Follow

If you keep doing the same things you will get the same results. Heard that before? You have to be prepared to let go of the past and let change in. To thrive, your creativity needs time, space and bravery: time to focus on what you love, headspace to grow and bravery to experiment. Allow yourself the headspace, and the motivation to clear your physical space will come.

Practical challenges, such as a leaky roof, can cause anxiety and won't help you feel ready to tackle your interior. Once you have invested mentally in the story you are about to create, you will also feel better able to tackle those nagging home jobs and do them right, so that they fit into the new home you are set on creating, not the one you are living in now.

We often get anxious clients asking, 'But how will I deliver? How do I make it happen? How will it work logistically?' as if the answer is the only thing that matters. But you need to master the art of freeing up your own creativity first. Yes, the 'how' is part of the creative process, but it isn't the place to start.

TRUE STORY

'I want to live in a submarine'

This is the story of a client who didn't use the majority of her space because she didn't feel comfortable in it. When we arrived at her lovely, but unfinished, home, alarm bells rang immediately. There were shelves with nothing on them, frames with nothing in them and a fear in the homeowner's eyes that we recognized instantly. First we were shown a tiny back room filled with bubble-wrapped artworks and piles of books and ornaments and photographs. When we settled down to talk over a cup of tea, it was in her favourite room, the kitchen, which had not been renovated since the 1960s. We were shown endless 'blingy' images on a laptop, collected to show us the type of interior she thought she should have. We paused for a moment, then asked, 'If you feel most comfortable in this room, which is modest, homely and ordered, why do you think you should have a luxurious layered interior with chandeliers?' There were unexpected tears for a moment and then a spark of honesty: 'The truth is I love order and function... I want to live in a submarine.'

We are not talking an underwater theme here! She meant a love of order and clean lines, with everything in its place – a submarine-like order. She felt trapped in a style that she thought was right for her area, her style of home and the expectations of her friends, colleagues and neighbours, but it wasn't right for her personally at all. It was a huge awakening for her to see that the only expectations she needed to fulfil were her own.

It's OK to want to live in a space where functionality is the primary concern. If you have friends who judge you on your interior, get new friends. Listen to your emotions and follow your instincts. They may be quiet at first, so nurture them.

Reading an Image

We once had a client with an extensive Pinterest board on kitchens, all with wildly different styles and colours. 'So you love bare brick?' we offered as a starting point. 'No,' they replied, 'I just loved the kitchen cabinet colour. I couldn't live with bare brick.' When looking at an image, it is important to interrogate the specifics of what you like and what you don't.

Photos are powerful because they hold so much information. It is all very well loving a photograph, but if you are going to benefit from it, you need to understand how it could relate specifically to your living circumstances. For example, you may love a shot of the interior of a palatial mansion, while you live in a modern flat – but what is it about the details that make it pop for you? Explore the images you love and work out what connects you to them before you file them away in an endless back catalogue. Try this out with the above photo of the kitchen at our Ewelme Road project in London, picking out what it is that you like and what it is that you don't.

A Home is a Journey, not a Destination

Creating a lovely home is a process that takes time and thought, so you need to stop chasing perfection if you want to enjoy the ride. *You* are the key to making living lovely and once you have the right tools, you will have the power to create a design that allows you to evolve and grow, adding things you love as you find them.

Whatever your nemesis, we have the antidote for you. We want to share with you our most powerful tool, the interior roadmap, which we've developed over years of working with clients on their homes.

It's important not to let the scale of what lies ahead get in the way of your creativity. The roadmap is designed to help you focus your ideas and it works no matter what stage you are at in a renovation, or in life for that matter. You don't need to know every detail of your home journey yet and of course there will inevitably be variations and surprises along the way. Treat the roadmap like a series of signposts along the bumpy road of interior design.

If you are living with others, whether a partner, family members or friends, you should all do the following exercise separately then come back together and share your roadmaps with each other. This is a great way to open up the communication so you can start to negotiate the main priorities of your home. More on this in the next chapter.

My Interior Roadmap

Take a pen and paper, not your phone; put that down
for a moment to engage in something analogue. Pick a pen colour
that makes you happy or enjoy the simplicity of pencil on paper.
Let yourself think freely and visualize your home as you want it to be,
a home that expresses who you are. What would it look like?

Your roadmap is simply a list of words about what you want to achieve
with your interior – a palette of colours, materials, functions and
feelings that form the bigger picture. Trust your gut and choose three
things for each category below that you feel drawn to.

Three colours

Three materials

Three functions

Three feelings

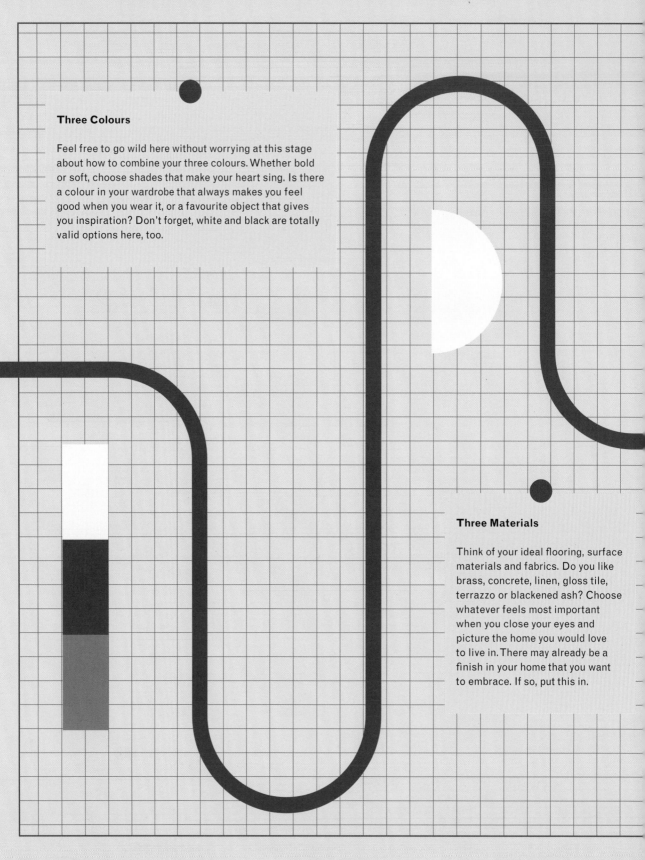

Three Colours

Feel free to go wild here without worrying at this stage about how to combine your three colours. Whether bold or soft, choose shades that make your heart sing. Is there a colour in your wardrobe that always makes you feel good when you wear it, or a favourite object that gives you inspiration? Don't forget, white and black are totally valid options here, too.

Three Materials

Think of your ideal flooring, surface materials and fabrics. Do you like brass, concrete, linen, gloss tile, terrazzo or blackened ash? Choose whatever feels most important when you close your eyes and picture the home you would love to live in. There may already be a finish in your home that you want to embrace. If so, put this in.

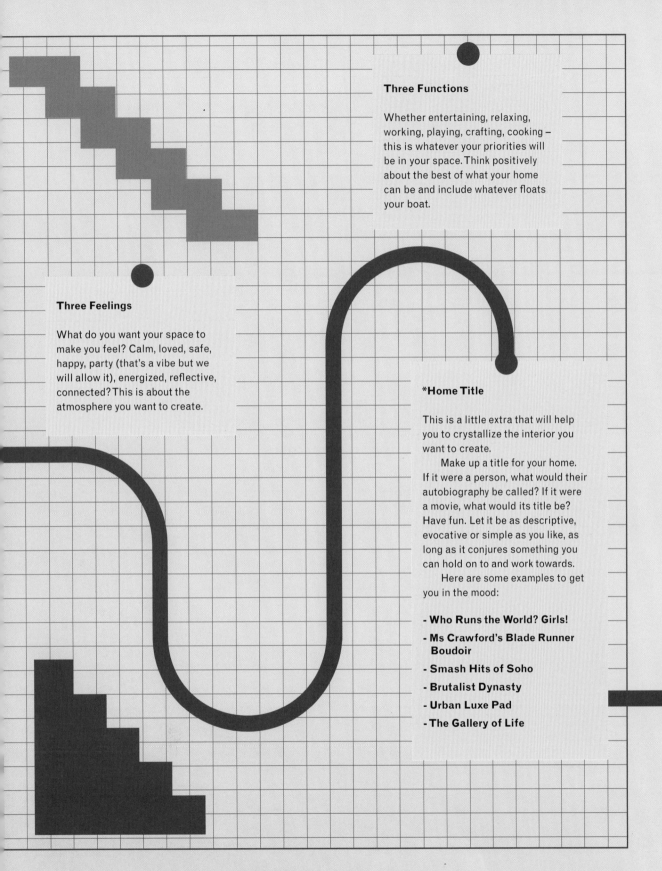

Three Functions

Whether entertaining, relaxing, working, playing, crafting, cooking – this is whatever your priorities will be in your space. Think positively about the best of what your home can be and include whatever floats your boat.

Three Feelings

What do you want your space to make you feel? Calm, loved, safe, happy, party (that's a vibe but we will allow it), energized, reflective, connected? This is about the atmosphere you want to create.

*Home Title

This is a little extra that will help you to crystallize the interior you want to create.

Make up a title for your home. If it were a person, what would their autobiography be called? If it were a movie, what would its title be? Have fun. Let it be as descriptive, evocative or simple as you like, as long as it conjures something you can hold on to and work towards.

Here are some examples to get you in the mood:

- **Who Runs the World? Girls!**
- **Ms Crawford's Blade Runner Boudoir**
- **Smash Hits of Soho**
- **Brutalist Dynasty**
- **Urban Luxe Pad**
- **The Gallery of Life**

Kelly Wearstler

'The most important aspect of a room is the spirit it conjures'

Our first featured designer on home is the queen of modern American interiors, Kelly Wearstler, who has been a hero of ours for many years. Her eclectic approach is always sophisticated, layered and relaxed, and her print designs and furniture pieces are as bold as they are playful. Her use of texture to create atmosphere is inspirational. You really don't know interiors until you get to know Kelly. Here we find out what home means to her.

My Interior Roadmap

My three key materials are stone, rich woods and patinated metals. Natural materials have so much soul. I adore all colours (so will not choose) but the three feelings I want my home to evoke are love, inspiration and passion.

What Home Means to Us

Home is where my family is. Home is love. The most important aspect of a room is the spirit it conjures and that holds true for what makes a house a home. Your home's environment is what gives you the right energy and inspiration to experience your own adventures.

I share my house in Beverly Hills with my husband, our two teenage sons and our three rescue dogs. It's where we live full-time and it is such a dream being there – we pinch ourselves daily. The house was originally built in 1926 as a Spanish colonial property, and was remodelled in 1934 by architect James E. Dolena. It has a rich Hollywood history and was once owned by Albert R. Broccoli, the producer of the James Bond films. The Broccoli family lived in our home for fifty years and there are amazing stories about the house during the golden years of Hollywood.

When we purchased our home we added about 370 sq m (4,000 sq ft) of floor space, as the house needed to be adapted to modern living. With an amazing energy and spirit, our home is incredibly peaceful and iconically Californian. We also have a beach house in Malibu that is situated right on the sand. During high tide the waves crash underneath the house and it feels like you are on a boat. It is a very special place where we enjoy quality family time on most weekends.

The furnishings in our house are by a melange of progressive contemporary furniture designers and artists, as well as including a selection of vintage furniture and unique curated finds from my travels. My most beloved possession is my teddy bear, Frank. Originally my grandmother's, he is my steadfast travel companion and has eyes fashioned from my grandfather's Navy uniform buttons.

Relaxing and Entertaining

I like to listen to all kinds of music, but I love hip hop, alternative, jazz, classical and opera. After a long day at work I like to take a hot bath, but when I'm with my family, snuggling together and watching a favourite movie is the best pastime. The house has an interior courtyard with the most beautiful garden and we love entertaining and opening up all the doors out to the garden. When we have guests over to visit it's a case of the more the merrier!

| CALICO | PINK | DARK BROWN |
| STONE | RICH WOOD | PATINATED METALS |

A residential project designed by Kelly Wearstler
in Los Angeles (above), and Kelly's Malibu home
(right and overleaf), with its sophisticated layers of
natural texture and vintage pieces.

Finding Your Path to a Free Home

Chapter One

Chapter Two

Cohabiting Without Compromise

Before you move on to the fun stuff – colour, materials and pretty things – you cannot ignore the importance of learning to live in your home with those you share your space with. Creating an interior that reflects all of you is key, so ignore the needs of those you live with at your peril. In this chapter you will learn that compromising needn't be the only way forward, if you can learn to successfully communicate and negotiate. By understanding and respecting not only yourself but also those you live with, you will find that your shared ideas take your interior down a path you could never have come up with alone – one that suits all needs and is brighter and better than any one person could have thought of.

'How do you do it?
Live together and work together?'
said everyone, all the time.

Freefall: Let the Communication Happen, Knowing You Will Catch Each Other Safely

We get asked how we live together more than any other question and it's true that problems with the interior you are trying to create so often stem from a conflict of ideas between partners, family members or friends. We can all learn to be good neighbours and cohabiters without sacrificing our needs and our dreams so that everyone is happy, but it takes good communication. Some people communicate visually and some verbally. We are all different and once you understand each other, you can start to talk the same language and move forward on your interior journey together.

Creativity is Conflict

OK, so we are not suggesting you should welcome arguments with your loved ones in order to make beautiful homes, but an acceptance of conflict during the design process is helpful and will make it less stressful for all of you. Often when it feels like you are swimming upstream, it's because you are actually headed in the right direction. Change is challenging. Don't be afraid of it and don't block it. Let it happen.

The Free Veto

To be treated with respect and used with caution, this is your trump card. You are generally only allowed to use this veto once and we hope you won't have to, except in very special circumstances. When a decision needs to be made on a room layout, colour or finish and their choice is going against every fibre of your being, that's when to use your free veto. It is for something that you simply cannot live with, a 'no way', that you get to use once in a blue moon with no discussion. The free veto is not to be confused with going out of your comfort zone and opening your mind to something new, so you really shouldn't need to use it if you are listening to each other's opinions, but it's there if you do. For use in an emergency only, because sometimes a veto is the only way.

PAGE 34

We used colour and touches of playfulness to help unite the styles of the newlywed couple who own this house in Hither Green, London (see page 43).

OPPOSITE

It takes grit to get through a renovation. We have been through many together.

Go on the Journey Together

Our interior roadmap from the previous chapter is a handy tool that can help you to understand the needs of everyone you live with and then negotiate which ones to prioritize.

When designing for our clients, we make a roadmap and then ask them to make a separate one of their own, so we can bring these together to create one definitive version. This process can take time. It can be the case that we come together and have six completely different colours, for example, and we then need to make a case for the three we've chosen. Some you win, some you lose, but the discussion often results in something wonderful! When doing this exercise with your partner or family, you should still end up with one definitive roadmap that is representative of you all, with only three answers for each category. This roadmap will become your bible throughout the design process. Every time you struggle to make a decision you can refer back to it as something you all agreed on and the answer should become clear.

Once you've got your roadmap in place, take time to work towards delivering your goals together. Whether you paint something, visit a lighting showroom or even commission something bespoke, doing activities together will help bring you closer and create an interior you are all invested in.

Refilling Your Creative Pool

Where does inspiration come from? We get asked this
as if it is something you either have or you don't. Inspiration
is not a talent, it's all around you all the time.

If the rut is real, take a moment to refill your creative pool
with some tried and tested inspiration sources. Bonding over new
ideas with those you live with is invaluable and you never know
whether the next big idea is just around the corner. Here are
some of our favourites to give you a creative boost.

Art Galleries – For creatives, galleries
can be as spiritual as churches. Whether
it's a colour you didn't know you loved
or a new perspective on what it is to be
human, you can be sure your creative
pool will be refilled after a moment with
the likes of Andy Warhol, David Hockney
or Olafur Eliasson (below).

↓

↑
Film – From Stanley Kubrick's *2001* to
Tim Burton's *Batman Returns* (above)
to *Sex and the City*, films are filled with
visual stimulation. If it makes your heart
beat faster on screen, you can apply
that same excitement to your home. Set
designs can be incredibly imaginative
and are a great source of inspiration.

Chapter Two

Theatres – Wherever you are in the world there is a form of theatre. At its heart, theatre is about telling stories, so seeing a show is a good way to reconnect with the story you're telling in your interior. Theatre buildings are themselves incredibly inspiring spaces, with great examples being London's National Theatre and Royal Opera House (below). One is all modern functionality, the other luxurious excess; both are spirit enhancing.

↓

Fashion – As art forms go, this one affects us every day of our lives. What you wear can define who you are. Visionaries like the late and great Alexander McQueen – heartbreaking in his pursuit of beauty – can make the ordinary magical and force us to dig deeper with our own creative ideas.

↓

↑

Shop Fits – With online sales rocketing, physical shops are now about experiences and some of their interiors can be insanely creative. Check out the likes of global brands Aesop (above) or Acne (below and below, left) for the most amazing inspiration.

Nature – From gardens and flowers to woodlands and coastlines, nature is the most primal inspiration of all. Don't ever feel silly for stopping to smell a rose or taking pictures of interesting clouds. If they speak to you, listen. So many of the colours we use in our projects come from nature.

↓

Music – Few things are more evocative than music and some of our favourites include Björk (below), Florence and the Machine, Miles Davis and Michael Nyman. Whichever artist you love, take time to listen, even if you just need a killer track to help you get that last section of wallpaper stripped. Music is a win for the creative process and can inform the mood of a space you want to create.

↓

Interiors are Without Gender

Think about colours in terms of the feelings they evoke and the way they interact in a space, rather than allowing yourself to be dictated to by social stereotypes. Colour is neither masculine nor feminine, nor are soft finishes 'female' and hard 'male'.

We are so over the 'pink is for girls and blue is for boys' thing. It's reductive nonsense. Throughout history the gendering of colours has fluctuated endlessly. Pink has been a male colour in the past, so when did it become exclusively female? Our home is predominantly pink and we love it, so there!

Free yourself from gender constraints and go with what makes you happy.

Free up the Physical Constraints

What kind of spaces do you have in your home? Which are shared, which are private, and can you find common ground?

If a room isn't working don't be afraid to change its function. If you work from home, it might be a better use of space to switch that large spare bedroom you only use twice a year with your small study, so you end up with a smaller spare bedroom and a larger office. Think carefully about how you occupy each space, who uses it and how often. There is always another way, you just have to be open and willing to try out new things. When it comes to defining functions, try to give each other a full win on one of your top priorities. If you each define your private spaces, it is then easier to identify the shared areas and work on these together. This doesn't mean you have to classify whole rooms as shared or private; even a defined area within a room counts.

What Happens When You Don't Compromise?

Sometimes the best ideas come with friction. Embrace it. In theatre, it's called dramatic tension and no great play works without it. Let the tension caused by trying to balance opposing ideas become a positive in the story of your interior. Maybe peanut butter and jam go together precisely *because* they are opposites (unless you have an actual peanut allergy and then feel free to use the veto, just this once). What is the peanut butter and jam of your shared interior?

In the interior below, which we designed for a young couple in Hither Green, South London (see overleaf), the juxtaposition of period features with contemporary furniture, eclectic belongings on bespoke shelving and the couple's favourite colours together in one scheme create a whole that is more than the sum of its parts.

Bring your favourite colours together, as
we did here in our Hither Green project.

Hither Green, London

This double-fronted period property in South London was in need of a personality injection. The young professional newlyweds who live here were struggling to agree on a design style for their first home together, with one loving all things contemporary and the other loving period features and antique pieces. We used dark floors to unite and ground the spaces, allowing us to be playful with our designs for this vibrant couple. Embossed wallpaper on the ceilings and under the dado rail in the hallway strengthen the impact of the period fireplace and coving, providing a perfect backdrop for eclectic contemporary lighting and furnishings. The spaces in this home have been brought to life with colour and design, taking them in a new direction that this couple both love.

Three Colours
Black, pink, 'Plasticine' blue

Three Materials
Plywood, marble, embossed wallpaper

Three Functions
Rejuvenate, entertain, grow

Three Feelings
Cool, energized, family

Home Title
Vibrant Classic Home

Chapter Two

PAGES 42–43

Off-white walls play a key role throughout, with bold colours
appearing in key areas, such as the nursery (page 43, top).

OPPOSITE AND BELOW

The impactful family bathroom, with double sinks and
modern fittings; modern design continues into the living space
on the ground floor, flooded with natural light.

Cohabiting Without Compromise

Calico Wallpaper

'Our home is minimally decorated, with wide open space for the kids to work on paintings or plant an indoor window-box garden'

Calico Wallpaper was founded in Brooklyn, New York, by husband and wife team Nick and Rachel Cope. They create stunning wallpapers that draw on traditional techniques and develop these into new processes that deliver textural, beautifully coloured backdrops for any interior. We have been friends with them for years and have loved following their design journey, having used one of their early print designs, Wabi, in our first ever interior design project. Their work is always beautifully realized with depth, scale and colour palettes that excite us.

Our Interiors Roadmap

The three key materials in our home are linen, ash and marble and our three key colours are schoolhouse white, manor house grey and all white. The three feelings we wanted our home to create are loved, safe and inspired, and three key functions for us are warmth, shelter and play.

What Home Means to Us

I live with my husband Nick and two children, Willow and River. We found our home on Craigslist when Nick and I were still dating, fell in love with it and never left. It's located on the Red Hook waterfront in Brooklyn and is an airy loft-style apartment in a beautifully restored 19th-century warehouse. There are original posts and beams throughout, which are numbered to indicate where coffee or grain used to be stored.

As we live near the water, we get a nice breeze when we open our windows. The open-plan layout allows the kids to play freely in the space and our interior is in a style conducive to creativity and exploration. For example, our daughter Willow has a rather elaborate easel on casters that she can move to different parts of the home depending on the light. We don't have fixed bedrooms for the kids. Instead we create temporary walls using sliding doors from the Sliding Door Company that divide the front space into two bedrooms. The same part of our home actually used to be our Calico Wallpaper office when we first founded the company in 2013.

The most beloved thing in our home is a necklace created by Lindsey Adelman that was traded in exchange for wallpaper.

Relaxing and Entertaining

To relax, I love to soak in the bath with a mud mask and a good book. We spend a lot of time at home, so our home environment is very important to us. It is minimally decorated and clean, with wide open space for the kids to work on paintings or plant an indoor window-box garden.

We are mostly listening to the kids' music these days, but luckily they have an affinity for the Beatles and Magic Dragons.

If our home were a movie, it would be the 1987 romantic New York classic *Moonstruck*.

SCHOOLHOUSE WHITE	MANOR HOUSE GREY	WHITE
LINEN	ASH	MARBLE

ABOVE

Calico's beloved cat, Irie, sitting pretty in front of their Wabi wallpaper in gold – a modern classic that enriches their space.

OVERLEAF

Calico's Aura wallpaper installed at the Casacor Miami exhibition in March 2019. The bold colours used in this organic ombre effect give this space strong personality.

Cohabiting Without Compromise

Chapter Three

The Tools
to Free
Your Home

There's infinite variety in the way we live and in the challenges presented by our homes. Now that you have created your roadmap and have a better understanding of sources of conflict with those you share your home with, here are some of our most potent tools that will hone your creativity and help you navigate your interior design path.

We are big believers in trusting your gut and we want to give you the confidence to feel free in not slavishly following rules. If you understand the basic framework of how the different elements of a space work, then you can learn to play with those elements. This chapter will help you on your journey as you create a home that feeds your soul and facilitates your lifestyle.

Tools Not Rules

Rules are bullshit. If we all followed the same rules in our interiors, design would stand still and we would all starve creatively and die of boredom. OK, that's a little dramatic, but you get the idea. We don't believe in interior design rules – we would prefer for you to use our 'tools' – just as we don't believe in following trends. We advocate 'slow interiors' that evolve and can be added to with things you love when you find them. Rules and trends can tie you in knots and restrict your ideas, but our tools can be used in an infinite number of different ways to unlock the potential of your interior.

This isn't a DIY chapter – our tools are for your mind, not your hands. We want to equip you with the mental tools to tackle your interior.

Craft Your Story

A home tells a series of stories about the lives of the people who live there, and strengthening and highlighting those stories will make a better home that enhances how you live your life.

Knowing how and where to start with your home is understandably difficult – a blank page can be daunting – but creativity is the best and most important starting point for any interior. Creativity thrives within constraints or, more accurately, parameters. If you know the audience (yourself and those you share your space with), know the building (its architecture, or 'the bones', as we call it) and know what you need from your space (the functions and feelings from your roadmap), then you already have a healthy set of parameters that mean you are no longer starting with a blank page. Use those parameters as a springboard and let them guide you. If you hate one or more of the parameters you are dealing with, then embrace that tension as a driving force that your design needs to work out. So much of design is problem solving, and making a home that works can feel like slotting a jigsaw puzzle together. That puzzle and the way you put it together will become a part of your home's story and will keep you connected to what you create.

'I am a human being, not an algorithm'

So you have a small space...
So you don't settle in one place for long...
So you are too settled...
So you are renting...
So you don't love the architecture...
So you have a strong-minded partner...
So your family run riot...
So you have six dogs...
So you hate curtains...
So you like flowers more than people...

Whatever your parameters, all of them
can be set free with creativity.
The same tools apply and we are going
to show you how to use them.

Respecting the Bones

Take time to define and assess the architecture of your home. What are its best and worst features? Are there elements you want to keep, such as mouldings, ceiling roses and fireplaces? What are the immediate challenges presented by your building?

Listen to your home. The architect built it that way for a reason and, if you let it, your space will tell you what it needs. If you live in a 1930s semi-detached house, don't try to turn it into a fake 18th-century manor. Respect the bones of what you have and some of the hard work is already done.

Do some research into the period in which your home was built. This is not to slavishly inform your choices for the interior, but to give you an understanding of where the building's structure and detailing have originated. This will free you to unlock the power of what already exists in your home and may turn what you previously thought of as unappealing details into virtues. Understanding something is so often the key to falling in love with it.

You may have a property in which the architecture appears to pose specific constraints, such as a narrow hallway, a problematic layout or a tiny bedroom: while those do need to be taken into consideration during the design process, don't let them take over from the start and restrict your creativity.

'Listen to the architecture, chances are it has something wonderful to say, and if it doesn't then you can fill it with your soul instead.'

PAGE 50

The modern-retro bedroom of our Birley Lodge project (see page 58).

OPPOSITE

The dressing room in our Victorian house is a modern twist on period bones, which places fashion influence at the heart of our home.

Chapter Three

A Well-Tailored Home

To help you to start thinking about all the different elements that go into making a home, think of it like a body and of yourself as its tailor, creating the perfect outfit to suit. This allows you to see the whole in its entirety, without focusing too much on individual elements. You know what suits your body, so get to know the bones of your house and create an outfit that brings out its best features.

Bone structure = Architecture
Heart = Kitchen
Head = Bedroom
Limbs = Hallways and connecting spaces
Eyes = Windows
Skin = Walls and floors
Hair = Window treatments
Clothing = Soft furnishings
Jewelry = Lighting
Shoes = Furniture

Interrogating the Architecture

Look away if you are an architect; this crib sheet is here to give a useful overview of different architectural styles. Your home will probably fall into one of these categories, each with its own beauty and idiosyncrasies. Understanding the bare bones will help you to design an interior that works with what you've already got.

Urban or New Build – This includes modern estates, apartments, tower blocks and anything that was built during a time of growth in a town or city, with space at a premium.

↓

Brutalist – Part of the 'Urban' category, but deserving of its own section as it is so distinctive. This mid-20th-century style is characterized by extensive use of concrete and a focus on function.

↑

Period – Each part of the world will have its own traditional style of architecture. Our home sits in this category, as it was built in 1870 and features brick walls and chimneys and ornate details around the windows and doors. For our purposes, this category covers anything pre-20th century with character and history.

Modernist – Industrialization led to new methods for construction in the first half of the 20th century. This style features new materials such as glass, steel and concrete, taking them to new heights. Often light and airy, this is where open-plan living began.

→

Postmodernist – This late 20th-century movement took Modernism and mixed it with pop culture. It combines styles and takes from all sorts of different eras and inspirations, just like a child in a sweet shop.

↑
Futurist – Think biophilic tower blocks, pod living, zero-carbon architecture and a focus on maximizing internal living experience without ornament or artifice.

→
Art Deco – Think 1930s Miami and Los Angeles. This is white, jade green, curves and beauty. It is clean-lined luxury at its best.

Country – This category covers country cottages, barn conversions, farmhouses and cabins. Found in natural or rural settings, these homes are often built using natural materials from their surrounding landscapes.

↓

↑
Industrial – When industry moved out of city centres, factory and warehouse buildings were left behind and taken over by creatives who pioneered 'loft living'. These are high-ceilinged spaces built with bare brick, rough steel and metal windows.

↑
Arts and Crafts – This was the beginning of the decorative movement in the late 19th century. Craftspeople took buildings to the next level, with naturally themed ornamentation. Think carved oak panelling, beaten copper and William Morris.

Birley Lodge, London

This project was about embracing this home's Brutalist architecture and running full-force down a glam 1980s rabbit hole. With its original teak floor-to-ceiling double doors, textured-concrete ceilings and large wraparound windows, we saw the potential of this interior immediately: it has great bone structure.

Bespoke upholstery, cutting-edge wallpaper and restored vintage lighting turn this into one luxury city pad that is full of charisma. The colour scheme was inspired by a trip to Milan design festival and the cult 1980s TV show *Dynasty* and perfectly suits the period of this apartment.

Three Colours
Royal blue, gold, terracotta

Three Materials
Teak (original doors), concrete (original ceilings), velvet

Three Functions
Relaxing, entertaining, working

Three Feelings
Glamour, luxury, warmth

Home Title
Brutalist Dynasty

Chapter Three

<u>OPPOSITE AND THIS PAGE</u>

Joan Collins at her most glam and Brutalism at its most bare:
put it together and we created this modern party pad that
oozes 1980s feeling.

<u>OVERLEAF</u>

When is a tired old vintage bedroom suite worth keeping?
When you reupholster it in deep blue velvet, of course.

The Tools to Free Your Home

Tilford Road, Surrey

We gave our own modern twist to this five-bedroom Arts and Crafts house in the countryside by using contemporary craftsmanship and bespoke elements. The challenge was to maintain the strong heritage of the architecture, while bringing the interior up to date with a fresh design take.

For the ground floor, we created a bespoke handprinted floral wallpaper (designed in collaboration with Studio Custhom) – our nod to William Morris's nature-inspired prints. Much of the original oak panelling, doors and pillars is left lovingly exposed, with a neutral base given to the rest of the home that lets the artworks and antique pieces shine. The centrepiece of the home is a bespoke brass and oak dining table, commissioned by us from British design brand NOVOCASTRIAN, with contemporary chairs by Ercol, and Liberty of London upholstered banquette seating, which gives another nod to the property's cultural heritage. The brass and black metal lighting in the hallways has a leaf motif that is entirely appropriate to the Arts and Crafts movement, yet with a modern wit, and, in the sitting room and music room, lighting by Pinch tells a strong story of craftsmanship that can be handed down through generations without ever taking itself too seriously. Bespoke encaustic tiles sit beautifully with the original deep-green glazed tiles of the fireplace in the music room and follow through into the family and master bathrooms, leading up to a modernized attic space that is part playroom, part movie room – an area for all the family to relax.

Three Colours
Forest green, pale pink, pale grey

Three Materials
Brass, encaustic tile, medium oak

Three Functions
Entertain, play, relax

Three Feelings
Freshness, cosiness, love

Home Title
Contemporary Arts and Crafts

OPPOSITE

Handprinted floral wallpaper gives impact in the entranceway and is a contemporary nod to the house's William Morris period heritage.

ABOVE LEFT AND ABOVE

The detailed arches in the stunning original hallway compare with the cosy modesty of the loft family room, with its kitchenette and cinema area.

LEFT

The original Arts and Crafts fireplace with a restored clock and complementary new glazed tiles.

Chapter Three

OPPOSITE

The elegance of modern craft brings the house's
period architecture to life with ease.

LEFT

Touches of modern sophistication pair with
vintage upholstery and a hand-knotted rug in the
design scheme for the living space.

BELOW

We created wraparound seating for this
bright dining area, with a bespoke table that's big
enough for all the family.

The Tools to Free Your Home

Focus the Function

A home that doesn't function is not free. A little work on focusing the function will go a long way to solving and refining problem spaces, so if you have a particularly dysfunctional room, don't just avoid it by buying more cushions. Take the time to tackle it. Save up if need be, but make it a priority.

Have you ever stopped to think, why do I walk into this room and does it fulfil that reason as well as it could? This reason is also the room's function and it needs defining and amping up in your design. Make that function as tasty as it can be, with the fewest ingredients, and you will feel an even stronger desire to enter the room. When the design of your space matches its function, it will bring you joy.

Are there rooms that you rarely enter or use fully? Have you ever stopped to think why? Could it be that you are stuffing too many functions into one space because you feel most at home there, or perhaps because you crave connection – to your garden, to your friends or to your family? This craving for connection is the reason open-plan spaces have become hugely popular in modern homes, but if you end up using one space all the time, it can start to feel cluttered and cramped. Are you using the space you have to its full potential? If it's open plan, your space may need zoning so that its openness has purpose.

Break it Down

A space can perform so many different functions, but only one or two really well. When you know what you want each room to *do*, you can choose the right finishes and objects and colours to enhance that. For example, if you want your bedroom to relax and calm you, this is its function and you need to design the interior to give your space the best chance of performing that role. Link your colour and layout choices to your functions.

This is where your sets of three roadmap keywords come into play. It's no good painting a bedroom red if your primary function is relaxation. Red may be your favourite colour, but it is vibrant and passionate. It will make you hot (not necessarily a bad thing for a bedroom), rather than cool and calm (after all, you did say your primary function, the thing you need the most from this space, was to relax, right?). Focus on that function and follow it through. We will explore working with colours and materials in more detail later in the book.

Find Your Light

Where does the natural light fall in your home at different times of the day and which rooms benefit most from it? Make the most of natural light by thinking about how the function of your space will work with its light levels. Darker bedrooms can be cosy, but a work space or a kitchen needs to be bright. A sitting room you mostly use in the evening may not need all the natural light, so could be in a darker part of the house. A frequently used dining area can often benefit from full light – perfect for lunches, daytime working from home or family events. Think about what works for you.

Lay it Out

Play with the functionality of your space by drawing out your ideas. A sketch, however rough, can reveal a solution to a challenging layout. Whether you prefer to use a simple digital program (there are so many out there now), or the humble pencil and paper, it helps to work out different ideas in a drawing before committing to the real thing. Measure out your space roughly – you are not working out precise measurements for final materials just yet – and play around with the positions of rooms and key pieces of furniture without making costly mistakes.

OPPOSITE

Transformational design features, such as this desk area in our home, can give focus to open-plan spaces and allow them to be multifunctional at different times of day.

The Tools to Free Your Home

Free the Flow

You know when you walk into someone's home and it just feels so good? That's flow. Creating a flow in your home, within the constraints of the space you have, will unlock the good vibes.

Step outside yourself for a moment and be that person walking into your home for the first time. How does the flow feel? Function and room layout are key. Go on a journey, looking at the way the spaces transition throughout, from the front door to the bedroom. Does the order of the rooms feel natural? Does it work for your life in your home? Try to put the functions (enter, entertain, work, cook, relax, bathe, sleep) in an order that reflects the journey you want to take each day.

You should also consider which rooms are more private and which are more public and have through-traffic. A private room, such as a bedroom, next to a front door can feel odd. You don't need to move all of your rooms around to achieve flow – that would be a huge undertaking – but by examining any issues with the existing flow, you will be better able to resolve them as you add layers to your design later. Think about your lifestyle and make the flow work for you.

Think About Flooring

Flooring is key to any successful space, so make sure you give it your attention. Enhance flow by connecting different spaces with one flooring choice, then use area rugs to define the functions of those spaces. A large rug under the seating area in your living room will focus that function and add a layer of cosiness. We will explore different types of flooring later on in the book (see Chapter Five).

Positioning Your Furniture

Next look at how to position large pieces of furniture within each space to get the most out of them. Don't let your furniture block the flow. Make sure pieces have enough space around them to allow free movement, although you can also use large pieces to break up open spaces and define different functions. Create vistas in a room that give the eye something wonderful to look at on the wall opposite the entrance, drawing you in.

'Broken-Plan Living'

Occasionally a soft break in a line is a great move. Get the flow of a property right and it isn't necessary to be entirely open plan. 'Broken plan' is a layout idea we see being used more and more as we crave connection. It's a step on from open-plan and requires knocking down fewer walls. To achieve it, try using glass partitions that divide your spaces, while retaining a visual connection, or go 'old skool' and use an archway to break a space up.

In the project shown opposite, we created a connection between the kitchen and living–dining area of this family home with an archway, which also maintains a subtle division between the spaces. The kitchen still feels connected, but the archway hides a little of its inner workings from the dining area.

Is there a wall blocking the flow
that could be removed?

Would your bathroom work
better upstairs than down?

Which room is currently
the heart of the house and
is it the right one?

Clean Lines

When assessing your space, try to think about how often the eye is distracted. Your eye line should flow as you look around a room. This means keeping it clean and simple and reducing elements that break up this line, so the effect is less jarring and more finished. Don't fight the existing structure of your space, if you can help it.

Clean up your interiors by taking note of the lines you have to work with, such as doorframes, windows and mouldings, then strengthening these with your use of colour and placement of mirrors and pictures to help avoid visual clutter. Where you have a choice, make it a conscious one to free the flow.

ABOVE

Make a virtue of structural breaks in spaces. An archway can create a soft connection between a kitchen and living–dining space, as it does in this home in Trilby Road, London.

The Throughline

Walk Your Space

Step into your front door and take yourself on a journey through your home. What feels right? Where can the flow be improved? Are all the functions working?

Draw it

Begin by drawing your layout. Categorize the different rooms and sketch out the pieces of furniture. Planning your ideas on paper will allow you to try out dramatic concepts without risky consequences.

Find Your Light

Natural light should be cherished. Rooms that get the most should be key parts of the home. Make darker areas the parts of the house you spend the least time in.

What Do You Need Each Space to Do for You?

Answer this question for each space, thinking about how to make the function work for you in your design.

Do One Thing Well

Decide what you want out of each space and keep your eye on that ball. A focused space will be so much more rewarding to you than a space that is trying to be all things to all people. Be brutal and push for one or two functions in each space.

Break it Down/Break it Up

Define your functions clearly through the layout of each space, thinking about clever uses of furniture, flooring and colours. You may want to break large rooms up with soft partitions to create a broken-plan space.

Tie Spaces Together

A seamless flooring or colour choice can create a throughline that will run through your entire home. Think about using a single colour on the woodwork, for example, that will pull all your home's different spaces together. More on this later.

Make Connections

Think about how you can make connections – between spaces or people and to the world outside. Seeing nature outside your window is one of the most basic human needs, connecting us to the world in which we live in a vital way.

Join the Dots

Develop your design to match the functions you identified and to create flow, and you'll be winning.

Use What You've Got

Live in the space you have. Use every part of it everyday. This might mean allowing certain spaces to be transformational, so the space is the same but the use changes: office by day, dining area by night, for example.

Placing Value

When it comes to the budget for your interior, it is important to be realistic with your expectations, but much more important to allow yourself creative freedom in the early stages, without letting budget constraints block your ideas. We often get asked, 'But how do I budget for that scheme and how will it work logistically?' Try to master the art of freeing up your own creativity, without letting worries get in the way. The most creative ideas can often be the most inexpensive, such as a clever choice of paint colour to define an area or a revived vintage find. First think about your vision for your home and then refine this to work within your means. If budget becomes an issue, it's much easier to hold on to the essence of your scheme if you set your goals for the space based on a story or creative idea you want to share. You will find that you make choices based on how well they tell the story, rather than the pricetag, and there are so many ways to tell a story.

Good Things Come to Those Who Wait

Define the pace of your project, as impatience can be costly. You may want to tackle your project in chunks that work for the budget you have and accept that the best things can take time. It's better to deliver one of your creative ideas fully than to miss the mark on all of them because you are trying to go full speed ahead.

Is it Adding Value?

Property value has been an obsession for a long time now, but shouldn't come at the expense of enjoying your home. Get excited about adding value to your lifestyle instead. Does it bring joy? Does it solve a problem? Does it create flow? Does it define an area? Property prices are not the only value. Live in the home you want now and address property value when or if you come to sell. How you experience your life is important, so prioritize it.

Think about what values you want to bring into your home, too. Does your design feature sustainable or recycled materials? Is it good for you? Some plastics and paints release chemicals into your home. Is that something you want to consider? Will your design help relieve stress and make your life a little easier? These are the kinds of questions we ask when we begin any new project. What are the problem areas? What can we add to this person's life? How can we enhance their spirit and bring them joy?

Ask yourself the same kinds of questions when you begin any new design project in your home and you'll create an interior with a strong sense of purpose.

'You define the budget, the budget does not define you.'

Hi-Lo Method

When you look at the bigger picture, you often find there is room for higher spends on individual items than you may be comfortable with in isolation. Balance more expensive items by making savings elsewhere in the scheme. You may do this naturally in the way that you dress, teaming that high street outfit with a pair of designer shoes. Your home can be the same. It's all about finding a balance.

In this project we chose a huge brass pendant light that was eye-wateringly expensive in isolation and made it possible on a modest budget by saving on other items. The light served all three open-plan spaces: kitchen, dining room and sitting room. We located it centrally above the table and used functional but inexpensive lighting elsewhere. We then found a vintage dining table and chair set online.

Try not to get tied up in the minute details of your budget, making every element sit in the same price point. If you find a piece that makes your heart sing, ask where else you can buy smart and save to make that star piece fit. Star finds can elevate the whole living experience, so make the budget flex creatively to your needs.

'We don't care where it is from or how inexpensive
it is, as long as it is painfully chic.'

ABOVE

This bold light in the dining area of our project in Brockley,
London (see page 146), is worth its weight, as it pulls together
several disparate spaces with a powerful statement of intent.

The Tools to Free Your Home

Sebastian Herkner

'The interior is something that is always in progress; it is never finished'

Internationally acclaimed product designer Sebastian Herkner has become known for his thoughtful use of materials and future-focused forms. Based in Offenbach, Germany, his studio has worked with global design brands Pulpo, Classicon, Moroso and Thonet, among others. We love his strong commitment to function and clever use of colour. He is also one of the nicest designers out there.

My Interior Roadmap

The three main materials in my home are concrete, ceramic tiles and wood. The three colours are white walls for art, dark grey to define areas and warm mint, and my three feelings are love, cosiness and comfort. My three functions are to charge batteries, meet friends and collect/store objects.

What Home Means to Me

I live in a new penthouse in the centre of Offenbach, Germany, with my husband, Manuel. We designed the floorplan and interior together to create a home for us both. It was great to have the opportunity to experience the building's construction and to decide almost all of the details of the final structure and interior. We sacrificed one 'kids' room' to get a good-sized master bathroom.

The main room has concrete floors and walls with a fireplace. The interior is a mix of my own designs, classic pieces and objects designed by friends. There are also souvenirs from our travels to Japan, Zimbabwe, Bali and Colombia. We both collect art from key artists of our generation, such as a Alicja Kwade. My favourite part of our home is our big main room, with an open-plan kitchen in the centre and Prouvé dining table; and my favourite piece is my Safari Chair by Carl Hansen, which is next to our huge window and fireplace. I love to sit there and watch the world outside and it's the best spot to look at our art collection. We also love our roof terrace, where we spend most or our time in the summer months having friends over for barbecues.

I travel a lot and spend almost every second or third night in a hotel somewhere. It's a good feeling to have a place to call home and to have someone with you. My interior is always in progress. It's never finished. Interiors are another way of expressing yourself and your feelings, interests and memories. It takes discipline to keep my home organized and tidy, but I think this is common. We have a storage room in the basement for our suitcases, winter wardrobe and Christmas decorations. The design of an interior is important, particularly the light and the colour palette, as well as the materials and the acoustics.

Relaxing and Entertaining

Why should I relax? I get bored when I have nothing to do. I love design and creativity in general, so when I have free time, I visit museums and cities, or we invite friends over. When we listen to music at home the music control is always in my husband's hand. I don't know why, it just happens! We listen to a mix of everything, but it's always related to the situation and our mood. We have a dining table for ten people, which is a good size for a dinner with interesting discussions.

Chapter Three

ABOVE

The extraordinary glass Container tables
designed by Sebastian for Pulpo.

RIGHT

The Oda light, also designed by Sebastian for
Pulpo, has become a classic.

WHITE	DARK GREY	WARM MINT
CONCRETE	TILES	WOOD

The Tools to Free Your Home

The Collar lamp is a pendant light designed by Sebastian
for Gubi that gives out a beautifully diffuse directional light,
perfect for a sophisticated dining area.

Chapter Three

ABOVE

Craft and industrial process are at the heart
of Sebastian's products, including this Pastille side
table for Edition Van Treeck.

The Tools to Free Your Home

Chapter Four

Decorative Joy

Now is the time to take out your swatch books and sample paint pots. This chapter is about creating layers of colour and pattern. If you understand the structure of your space, you're now ready to discover how to play with decoration and learn new things about yourself as you do so. You may find that you call yourself a colour lover but have no colour in your interior, or you call yourself a pattern person, but have not put any pattern into your living space. We want to give you the freedom to play outside your comfort zone and consciously fill in your clean lines with elements that bring you happiness.

Decorative joy is not about 'wow factor' and token statements. It is about immersing yourself in a home environment that strengthens your sense of self and opens up new possibilities for the way you live your life. Let the fun begin.

Colour as a
Starting Point

Colour can be so evocative and is a wonderful starting point for a design. There are plenty of great places to find colour inspiration, from your mother's hair colour to your first favourite pair of shoes or an album cover you love. But colour can also be as divisive as it is unifying, so how do you avoid colour conflict? Interrogate your choices and learn to tell stories with colour, so that all who live in and experience your space can appreciate your colour story with you.

Unpicking your relationship with colour will help you to understand it better. Are you someone who is naturally drawn to colour or do you find it difficult? Perhaps it doesn't interest you or you take it for granted? To call yourself colour-averse (we hear this phrase too often) is to say you are life-averse, as colour is around us all the time. Even a crisp white snowscape is actually full of colour if you look for it: the clean blue of the ice, the pink hue of the afternoon sun reflecting off the snow. Let us not forget, too, that shades of white and grey – commonly called 'neutrals' – are still full of different colours. A beige may have hints of green and grey in it and a warmer tone may contain gold and rose. Colour is in everything we see.

How you use colour can transform the way you live in your home and make your experiences of everyday life better. Begin to think about colour as a positive force and explore its impact on your interiors. If you love grey then feel happy and confident in that; if you are passionate about pink, embrace that and run with it. The next step is to make conscious choices about how and where you use colour. Start by asking yourself these questions.

Who is it for?

Will the colour be enjoyed by everyone who comes to your home or is it intended for a private space like a bedroom? Is it for an adult space or for children? Consciously thinking about these things will help you to decide where to put the colour.

Where is it for?

What does the architecture want colourwise? Are there surfaces such as brick, concrete or wood that your colour choices need to complement? Are you in the countryside or in an urban space? Are there colours from your home's setting that will create connections? Do you deliberately want to play against that to give the design edge?

What is it for?

Is the space for sleeping, playing, eating, initial impact, morning energy? Pick a colour to aid the function of your room. The choice will be personal to you, as we all have different feelings and associations with colours, so don't feel you have to adhere to particular rules. It's a good idea to link back to your roadmap when thinking about your room's functions and how they relate to the colours you like. Here's an example:

SLEEPING	RELAXING	HAPPY

Confidence
is Magic!

You know that person who walks into a room wearing a killer red dress and they make it look like the most effortless, sophisticated thing, without even trying? The room is theirs and the dress is not a wacky statement or a bold move, it is just them. They are just wearing it, so what?

It is all down to confidence, and that comes from within. Compliments give a momentary buzz, but confidence is not about needing validation. It is about making choices based on your own story and how you understand your home, those in it and the way you want to live. Confidence is something you feel as soon as you walk into a home that has been freed. If you can pull this off with your interior, it will make for a thrilling design. Start to create some magic.

Modern Rainbow

No matter the colours you are using, putting a simple set of constraints in place can help you tackle a space more creatively. Here we show you two modern ways we have used all the colours of the rainbow, without ever tipping over into wacky cliché.

The Rainbow Room

This space is a concept (that staircase isn't going to take you anywhere), but it features a great colour idea that can be applied in a real setting. We took on the challenge here of creating a space that embodied our belief that you can use colour alone to define a space. The palette is all the colours of the rainbow, using our preferred shades. The yellow is pale lemon – fresh as you like – the pink is pastel perfect and the

green errs towards the emerald. There are infinite tones and shades to choose from, so feel free to play with your palette. Colour is about expression and joy.

In this design, we used lots of different effects, from the handpainted terrazzo floor to the striped column, which was creating using masking tape. Orange is a challenging colour for us. Here, we hand-applied gold leaf to an orange canvas to introduce texture and interest. Finally, we created the illusion of depth by continuing the staircase up the walls with a painted mural, again using masking tape as a guide.

Chapter Four

The Loveseat

Here we applied our rainbow concept to a piece of furniture that we reimagined for a new generation. The blended colours – from pastel lilac to neon yellow to indigo blue – on this iconic handmade Ercol loveseat would give any room a modern colour hit. You don't have to bring a different colour to every element of a room. Sometimes one or two key pieces are all you need to enliven your space with good vibes.

The important things here were getting the right proportions and carefully choosing the best positions for the different colours. Some colours don't love each other, so we took time to allow each colour to interact in happy combos.

When thinking about your space, look out for pieces that bring the colour in, whether an artwork, a rug or a bold statement armchair.

PAGE 78 AND BELOW

Our limited edition colourway of the iconic Ercol loveseat raised money for Pride and Stonewall.

Modern Monochrome
Ms Crawford's Suite, 2049

This all-pink scheme takes the simple starting point of one colour and then pushes it to the next level. The vibe we wanted to create was luxe with a tongue-in-cheek nod to futuristic movies, such as *Blade Runner 2049* (2017). The slim black light fittings ground the look to stop it from floating away. If Joan Crawford were an AI in the near future, perhaps this could be her boudoir. Apply the monochrome look to any space for a bold touch of class. (Commissioned by Hillarys, designed by 2LG Studio.)

Pattern People

Pattern is universal. We all connect the dots of things we see and turn them into patterns, from stars in the night sky to clouds, trees and the configurations of flower petals. No wonder we are drawn to patterns in our homes, too – from geometrics, florals and marbling to stripes, dots and interlinking animals (such as this wallpaper inspired by our dog, Buckley), the list goes on.

Patterns can also trigger memories, whether it's grandma's house with its kitsch borders in every room or the patterned coat of the first person you fell in love with. Even an old and fragile scrap of wallpaper you find under layers of paint in your new home can connect you to something human, unique and expressive, giving your space a story.

When used with confidence, a pattern draws you in to a space and gives your room depth and impact, so it's important to think about where you want to put it. Don't just throw it into the mix with abandon: it deserves more of your time. If you love a pattern, but don't know how or where you want it yet, that's OK, too. The solution may reveal itself later, and even if it doesn't, your pattern can always appear in small doses as cushion covers, like a little gift for those who linger on your sofa.

Architects are often afraid of pattern or even snobby about it, seeing it as layer without function that distracts from a building's authentic materials. In contrast, interior designers use pattern to add decorative flair and layers of luxury, bridging the gap between function and decoration. The function of pattern is to add depth and beauty, bring connection and create joy. If you have identified a pattern that brings back fond memories, creates new ones or simply lifts your spirits, then it is worth adding into your design.

CASE STUDY

Adam Nathaniel Furman
Architect, Scholar, Designer and All-Round Lovely Gent

This is one architect who is not averse to pattern. Adam Nathaniel Furman is a visionary who embraces pattern with an infectious vigour. His designs (above) are blazing a trail for architects and designers of the future.

Adam on Pattern

'While being educated at university in architecture and design, surrounded, swamped and almost drowned in a sea of miserable techno-minimalism and functionalist dogma, I came to fall in love with the creative possibilities of patterns. I was like a parched, starving man in a desert who has suddenly, miraculously, come upon an oasis full of melons, apples, buffets, barbecues, George Michael, music and pina coladas. Like clothes, like make-up, like highly composed and fabulous photographs of ourselves – these things that allow us to become something new and more dramatic, to communicate feelings within us that our bodies alone cannot, or just to feel the kind of glamour and confidence that we would never otherwise feel – patterns bring inert materials to life. They can dress up the most boring piece of MDF and turn it into a drag diva telling bitchy jokes, or turn a plank of plywood into a magic beam of queer chinoiserie that would lift the spirits of even the most miserable of minimalist aesthetic puritans. A deceptively thin "surface effect", pattern can bring depth and magic to whichever material it is applied to, and turn the most banal of interiors into cabarets of deliriously delicious delight.'

Focus on Print Design

Every interior tells a story, and here is one of our home stories that also gives an insight into our print design process. A humble detail that may seem like nothing can lead to something wonderful, if you keep your eyes open and your roadmap in mind.

Once we had spent all of our initial budget on fixing the roof of our new home, restacking the chimneys, rewiring and putting in central heating (all the boring bits), the downstairs bathroom was the first space we designed. This small and perfectly contained project would set us off on the creative path of redesigning the whole property.

While stripping layers of old paper and paint in the bathroom, we found a totally ugly scrap of 1950s ditsy floral wallpaper and were inspired to set ourselves a challenge we could not resist: to take a retro floral pattern and turn it into something for our new home. We had been working with Studio Custhom for a while, specifying their prints for our residential client projects, and had already become friends. This was the perfect opportunity to work with them.

What started out as a bespoke print for our new space ended up as a three-piece wallpaper and fabric collection that we showed with Studio Custhom for Ligne Roset at London Design Festival and New York Design Week. Who knew a tiny scrap of paper could start an entire collection?

We love to collaborate, perhaps because of our theatre training and careers on the stage, and are naturally drawn to working with others and exchanging different ideas. Work with people you love, with skills beyond your own, and the results can be so much more than you ever imagined.

OPPOSITE

Our Forest Hill print collection designed in collaboration with local friends, Studio Custhom, began life as a commission for the downstairs WC at our Design House.

RIGHT

From humble beginnings. This installation for London Design Festival at the Ligne Roset store features our print design on the iconic Slice chair by Pierre Charpin.

BELOW

We shot these decorative obelisks in a local gem, the glasshouse at the Horniman Museum in South London – a place of beauty.

Decorative Joy

Dimore Studio

'Part diary, part biography, our home includes the furniture and objects we have collected over time'

We adore Emiliano Salci and Britt Moran of Dimore Studio. A major influence in the interior design scene, their transformational show apartment forms the centrepiece of Milan's Fuorisalone – arguably the most important design show on the planet – year after year. Their work combines a deep passion for the past with contemporary print designs and a touch of theatre. Atmosphere, created by music, lighting and evocative curations of objects, plays a dramatic role in all of their work. They are also the kings of 1930s Art Deco revival, with a heavy dose of 1970s style and an Italian edge that is always filled with emotion.

Their home is key to their working life together and their private lives as friends and cohabiters.

bathrooms, two bedrooms, one guest room, one dining room, one living room, one laundry room and two corridors.

We were looking for a house with a 1930s feel that had been left untouched and we fell in love when we saw the interiors, the boiseries (carved wooden panelling), the flooring and the decorated chimney. The lack of a lift is the only part of the home we don't like. We love the 1930s architecture, and the most beloved thing in our home is a collection of old Japanese mirrors (a gift from Emiliano to Britt).

Part diary, part biography, our home includes the furniture and objects we have collected over time and, as per our projects, we have combined historical and contemporary materials, metals and textures.

Our Interiors Roadmap

The three materials that mean home for us are wood, brass and lacquer. Our three key colours are green, mustard yellow and orange-brick red, and the three feelings we want from our home are peace, cosiness and well-being. Finally, our three key functions are to relax, listen to music and eat.

What Home Means to Us

We live together, though we are not a couple. One of our rules is not to take work home, but we do end up discussing upcoming projects. Our flat is 220 sq m (2,370 sq ft), with a 250 sq m (2,690 sq ft) terrace. It comprises a kitchen, two

Relaxing and Entertaining

Home is a refuge from the hectic life we lead, and a place where we like to entertain small groups of friends. Eight dinner guests is an ideal number for us to be able to enjoy the company and the talk. The music we listen to at home depends on the mood. We like music and we play it constantly.

If our home was a movie it would be *The Garden of the Finzi Continis* (1970), based on the novel by Giorgio Bassani and directed by Vittorio De Sica.

| GREEN | MUSTARD YELLOW | ORANGE BRICK |
| WOOD | BRASS | LACQUER |

ABOVE AND RIGHT

Dimore Studio's design for the Hotel Saint-Marc in Paris evokes classic European cinema.

OVERLEAF

Britt and Emiliano's home, an apartment in Milan's Viale Jenner, has breathtaking drama.

Decorative Joy

Chapter Four

Freestyle: Getting Playful with Combos

New territory is enlightening if you approach it with openness – the essence of play. Get playful with how you layer colour and pattern and don't be afraid to make mistakes. For every mistake there's a moment of genius, so treat unexpected results as a learning experience.

Earlier we talked about moodboards and their tendency to trap you into specifics if employed too early in the process, but now is a great time to try moodboarding some layers.

Decorative Function

Remember that you are trying to create a 'feeling', or atmosphere, in each space that complements its function. Try to connect the function of your space to a decorative combo that will enhance this atmosphere. For example, if you want your living room to feel cosy, think about how you can combine colour and pattern to achieve this.

Creating Themes

We are not talking about old-skool ideas of theming spaces, as in the theatre-inspired dining rooms, Aztec living rooms and mermaid-themed bedrooms of makeover TV shows. When we talk about themes, we mean subtle connections, not gimmicks. A colour or a pattern can be a great way to connect spaces and draw the eye through your home. In our house, we used the colour of the woodwork to connect the spaces. Electric blue is also a theme that appears in small surprise doses throughout. For example, you may want to connect a pattern on the walls of your entrance hall (hallways are a great place for bold patterns, as they are transient spaces) to a rug in your living space off the same corridor. This is a simple way to draw the eye into your space and create flow.

Chapter Four

The Mud in the Water

We use this phrase a lot and we will try to explain it, but it's really a feeling.

When we put together a scheme and stand back, sometimes one element stands out, killing the vibes and softening the design's edge. This is the mud in the water. It could be a colour, a texture or a finish – anything that stops the clarity of the design from coming together. For example, in a black and white scheme it could be something as simple as a cream rug. The mud in the water may only become obvious at the final stages of designing your home, but this is why looking at the elements of your design on a moodboard in the early concept phase is so useful and can save you time and money in costly mistakes. Editing your ideas is part of the process. Never be afraid to get rid of the mud in the water if you spot it.

Getting Proportions Right

You can improve the visual proportions of a long, thin room with furniture, colours and materials. Spaces can be made to feel wider by using a bold colour on the smallest end wall to bring the wall visually closer to you and stop the room feeling like a corridor. Light colours on flanking walls will make them recede. Place the largest piece of furniture, such as a bookcase, storage wall or large sofa, at the far end of the room to help make a narrow rectangular room look more square.

Lay it out on one of the many floorplanning apps or programs available out there or just on good old-fashioned paper before you begin, to plot out your throughline and how best to use your space.

Let it Happen

Try out decorative moodboards on a table using fabric samples and paint colour chips. Indulge in this, taking time to lay out your favourite colours and patterns. The safe environment of a moodboard will often bring out some special combination you would not have otherwise thought of.

Layering

Your design may involve multiple layers, and it can help to think of these like a perfume, with each forming a base note (the underlying concept), middle note (the heart of the design) or top note (the accents that grab attention). Your layers may get more or less complex as you add accent colours and edit patterns. Try mixing small- and large-scale patterns and uniting these with a complementary colour, or try combining several clashing colours and unifying them with a complementary pattern – even stripes upon stripes. Trust your gut and choose combinations that excite you.

OPPOSITE

The woodwork in our Design House continues a colour theme throughout, as do circular mirrors, which appear in various spaces.

ABOVE

Floorplanning apps and programs are a great way to help visualize your design. Here is an example floorplan from one of our projects.

Decorative Moments

Simple details can be used in any space to create moments of decorative joy. Here are two examples we love that are easy to try in your home.

Decorative Tape

This is such an easy and inexpensive way to update a space! Washi tape, now widely available online, is basically a heavy-duty sticky tape that you can use on your walls. It can be used as a border or, as we have done here, in varying depths and colours to create a bold graphic scheme. Get creative and remember that if you hate it, you can remove it without damaging your surfaces. It's perfect if you are renting or if you want a room that can easily transition.

Here we have added layers to create a fresh take on a Scandi industrial vibe for this family home in Standring Rise, London. The 1960s property was a white box, with no features to speak of. This home has been transformed by decoration and given new life for the young family who live here. We added personality with hand-applied decorative washi tape in bold, area-defining diagonals. The large corner sofa creates a snug for all the family to watch movies or a place to entertain in the summer, and a vintage sideboard, with a new coat of green chalk paint, gives the space a strong colour identity.

Simple Stripes

Handpainted stripes are also a great way to add a classic decorative layer to a space. Here are two examples of spaces we designed – Trilby Road (left) and Clapham Common (below) – that we have brought to life using only masking tape and a little patience. Choose a strong contrast colour for your stripes to create maximum impact with minimal effort. There is nothing more satisfying than peeling off the masking tape and seeing the finished result.

Don't Forget
Your Ceilings

Revisit the fifth wall, the forgotten expanse above
your head. We often remind ourselves to look up at the
architecture when walking the streets of a new city or at
the stars when enjoying a night in the great outdoors, but not
so much inside our homes. Ceilings are one of the biggest
decorative expanses in any room, but they are often painted
white and then just ignored. They are another opportunity
to craft your space, so think carefully about how you might
use your fifth wall in your scheme.

Ghosts of Ceilings Past

You've just removed some vintage wallpaper from your ceiling
to begin your redesign, but maybe those past owners were on
to something after all. This may sound mad, and we are not
trying to suggest that Artex was a great idea and woodchip
should be revisited, but retro-inspired wallpaper on ceilings
doesn't have to be just a kitsch throwback. Patterned and
colourful ceilings can impact a space enormously.

Lift it Up or Bring it Down

Look at the proportions of your room. Is the ceiling height
high or low? How can the treatment of your ceiling shape
the feeling you want to create in your space? Low ceilings
benefit from pale colours and gloss finishes that bounce light.
Higher ceilings can take patterns, murals and bold colours.
If you want to make a space feel homely – a living room, for
example – try spreading a colour from the top section of the
walls on to the ceiling, bringing the ceiling down a little. Use
existing lines – the windows or a picture rail – to bring the
ceiling colour down in a visually effortless way.

Like it Grew There

Create drama in a small space by using rich colour on
your ceiling, as we did in the dressing room shown opposite
(top, left). We added an oversized rippled ceiling rose and
painted the ceiling in a burgundy shade that matches the
pendant lampshade. Using one colour across these three
elements gives the impression that the light is growing out
of the ceiling.

Take Pattern to the Next Level

Because ceilings sit above your eyeline, using a patterned
wallpaper can give life to a space without being overwhelming.
In the two examples shown opposite (bottom, left and right)
we added elegance to a dining space (left) with beautiful blue
wallpaper – a talking point for any dinner guest – and used
a patterned paper of our own design (see page 88) in this
small ground-floor bathroom (right).

LEFT

The pendant light inspires the deep-red ceiling colour
of this dressing room with added drama.

BELOW LEFT

We designed this highly decorative dining room with
complementary patterned wallpapers from our collection
for Graham & Brown on the walls and ceiling.

BELOW RIGHT

We used this wallpaper we designed across the
ceiling and down the walls for an all-encompassing
impact in a small space.

Chapter Five

Materiality: Feeling Space

The materials you choose give your space both texture and atmosphere. A home filled with considered materials that interact with each other, and with you, is much more than the sum of its parts.

From recycled plastic and reeded glass to classic marble and natural textiles, the world is your oyster when it comes to the myriad material options available, but don't feel overwhelmed. Your approach to materials should be playful and inquisitive. Respect them and use them to tell your story. As with patterns and colours, you can bring joy in the way you layer materials, or by creating a throughline with one strong material choice.

The word 'finishes' implies a final layer in your renovation, but this isn't the end. Materials will patinate and soften over time as they live with you and, as with colour and pattern, a material can just as easily become a starting point for your design as it can be a finishing touch.

The Power of Texture

Texture is as essential as colour in interiors. A wonderful way to introduce atmosphere, it can help bring even a very muted colour palette to life.

Texture can be subtle or bold and in-your-face – think deep-pile rugs and exposed brick walls – so bear in mind both the functions of your spaces and how they should make you feel.

Craft the atmosphere you want and let textures play off each other to create interest and depth. For example, you might think of your bathroom as a sanctuary of cleanliness, which may lead you to choose high-gloss finishes or reflective surfaces. If you want comfort in your living room, you might choose soft textures for your furnishings, such as washed linen and velvet, and if you want to carpet the floor, think about

which type of carpet: sisal is very different from bamboo silk, both in durability and in the way it feels underfoot.

Materials can also help to ground a scheme. For example, if the interior you are creating is playful and light throughout, try using some contrasting materials in the mix that will keep it real, such as black hardware. If you are creating a fresh pastel scheme, you might try subtly grounding it by using bronze, mid-oak or another material with a deeper natural colour in order to stop the scheme from floating away. Remember that every surface holds power.

ABOVE

Hand-cut zellige tiles create a beautifully tactile surface on our chimney breast, with their tonal pinks and undulating glazed surface.

ABOVE

This newly built extension is connected to the original parts of the property with the use of these weathered reclaimed doors to soften the transition.

Power Combos

A room that is all matt and soft or entirely shiny and hard will often be less interesting than a scheme that mixes all four together. Start simple and build up, thinking about how you want your textures to interact and balancing them to enhance their power. You know we aren't ones for rules, but here are some killer combos to bear in mind.

Matt and Gloss

Think paint, tiles, wood and varnish. Never underestimate the impact of different levels of sheen in a room to create interest, soften hard lines and reflect light. There is also more to paint than just colour. Think about texture and finish as well. We love to play with matt and gloss paints, sometimes even in the same shade, and have painted ceilings in our home in gloss pink and the walls in matt pink, for example – the effect is wonderful and really unusual. The days of 90s gloss-painted skirting boards and doors may return sooner than we thought.

Soft and Hard

Balance your space. Hard surfaces are necessary in a kitchen, but think about softening them with wooden furniture, paper lighting or an upholstered window seat to stop the room from feeling uninviting. Equally a soft space, such as a bedroom or living room, may benefit from some hard edges to add sophistication and give structure. Surfaces also affect acoustics. Hard materials echo, while softer ones absorb sound, so thinking about what you want to use your space for will make choosing the right textures a little easier.

Rough and Smooth

Think linen and velvet or raw and polished. Textures of fabrics and surfaces can work beautifully in contrast. For example, you could try deep-pile rugs on poured concrete floors, bare wood with polished plaster or mixing large-weave slub linen with smooth cotton velvet.

Plant and Mineral

Naturally occurring materials always look beautiful. If nature did it first, you can bet on it being a wicked combo, so don't hesitate when it comes to building a scheme that embraces plants, stone, wood and linen. Soft with hard, matt with gloss, it's already out there in the natural world, so get involved. Embrace your inner nymph and surround yourself with all that is green and good.

Choosing the Right Material for the Job

Materials need to work. They have a job to do, fulfilling a function as well as giving you a rich sensual experience. Yes, we did just use the word sensual (sorry, not sorry). Whether a splashback, bathroom tile, cabinet door or door handle, ask yourself does it need to withstand heat, water, stains, heavy footfall? Once uses, stresses and strains are identified, you'll make your life much easier. The right material used to the best of its ability will always reward you.

You don't want to be stressing over tiling choices last minute. Make strong, informed decisions early on that free you to make the fun decisions later. A little research goes a long way and suppliers are usually happy to help with any questions.

Be Inquisitive

Being conscious in your decisions will give you confidence, so do take your time over more transient materials like upholstery or painted furniture. A piece of upholstery may not outlive a brick wall or solid wood floor, but that does not mean you should make a throwaway choice. Give it your love and it will reward you for however long it's there. We have found original pieces of fabric in our house that we love, in spite of their age and level of damage. They still capture something valuable that we will carry into our home's next phase.

Get to know the specific qualities of materials and where they are best used. This task can be daunting, but use your roadmap to focus on the specifics of your project and keep you on track. Focus on your functions and the interior story you are trying to tell. This is important when thinking about not only the bones of your space – walls and floors – but also soft furnishings and hardware, such as handles. All these elements must combine to make a coherent interior.

Floors

The floor is one of the biggest expanses in any room and therefore a huge opportunity. As we've already seen on page 71, flooring can be a powerful way to create a throughline in your property, pulling together disparate spaces and giving your home instant flow. When choosing flooring to run throughout your home, try to find a material that will work for you in a variety of spaces, from kitchen to hallway to living room.

Walls

From bare plaster to paint, wallpaper and concrete, there are many options to choose from for your walls. When making your selection, think about the traffic in that space. Will the wall surface need to be durable? Is it protected inside an alcove and can therefore have a more delicate finish? If you're in a situation where you need to replaster all your walls and you are already back to bare brick, would you prefer to make a feature of this or might you want to consider using plywood to clad the walls instead of plasterboard?

Surface Materials

Make sure to research the materials you are considering and ask suppliers about suitability for the area in question. The right material in the right place will last longer and do the job you want it to do. For kitchen worksurfaces, make sure it is heatproof and as stainproof as possible. Marble is a beautiful material, but certain types can stain, making them unsuitable for many kitchen applications. Choose Carrara marble or granite over more decorative, but porous, slabs, leaving more ornamental pieces of marble for wall cladding or side tables. Composite stone has added durability for a busy family home.

Tiling

Tiles come in many finishes, shapes and sizes, making them fun, and sometimes frustrating, to choose. Think about maintenance. Will your tiled area need frequent cleaning, will it get muddy, does it need to be waterproof (such as a shower area) or is it purely decorative (such as a fireplace)? Natural stone can be beautiful, but will need sealing. Glazed tiles offer a wonderful durable surface, but think about the colour of your grout lines. Mosaics are stunning, but add to installation costs as they must be done correctly to be durable. Ask the advice of your supplier and choose tiles that keep you smiling because you don't live on your hands and knees scrubbing and resealing them.

Hardware

We're talking about light switches, plug points, door handles and cupboard openings – all the things you touch on a daily basis. You would be amazed how many people overlook these and choose go-to white plastic or stainless steel, so take a moment to think about how often you connect with these materials. If you have put thought into them, you will feel the difference. Don't be afraid to mix metals. 'Matchy-matchy' is not the only way to design and a considered mix of metals that complement each other can be gorgeous.

Soft Finishes

From upholstery and curtains to rugs, carpets and even padded headboards, textiles offer a whole world of materiality that we are passionate about. You will often find us in a store's fabric department touching all the different rolls and swatches. It is so satisfying spending time getting to know the qualities of different textiles. Some fabrics are perfect for heavy use (on family sofas, for example), while others may be more suited for occasional use on a statement bedroom chair. You can make a big impact with just a small amount of luxury fabric for a cushion cover, while you may want to use a more cost-effective option, such as natural linen, for curtains and other larger expanses.

Sustainability at Home

We are now more 'woke' than ever and it's no longer an option to turn a blind eye to climate change and sustainability. The more you know about the challenges facing our environment, the more responsibility you have to make mindful choices, and this includes how you choose to design your home. Select materials that help our planet, and your living space will make you feel better. Here are some great options.

Wonderful Wood

Wood has many undeniable qualities and is the most incredible resource that should be embraced more in our interiors, when grown sustainably. As a material, it connects us to nature, is strong and durable and comes in a huge variety of finishes and colours, such as this headboard at Trilby Road, London. As a material, it is also incredibly beautiful and wood grains drive us crazy with love. Felling and growing trees sustainably absorbs carbon dioxide from the atmosphere, helping to combat climate change.

Bamboo

Fast-growing and sustainable, bamboo is a great go-to choice for flooring, furniture and accessories. Some bamboo-based materials are highly processed with bad chemicals, so go for those that use the raw materials in the most eco-friendly way.

'"Be the change you want to see" is a phrase we come back to
time and again when choosing materials.'

Cork

With its rather kitsch reputation, cork has struggled
to break through into the mainstream, but it must not be
overlooked as a 70s throwback. Waterproof and sustainably
grown, it has endless applications and can be used for flooring,
wall coverings, pots and even to make cork leather. We used
cork flooring in our Trilby Road project, shown below.

Recycled Plastic

Advances in the development of new recycled materials
are becoming more exciting all the time. There is so much
discarded plastic on our planet that is not going anywhere
soon. In the long term, we need to learn to live without single-
use plastics – the sooner the better. Recycled-plastic surfaces
can be wonderfully colourful and textural and we have used
these in kitchens and bathrooms, such as this one at Granville
Park (see page 112), to great effect.

Reclaimed Materials

We all throw so much away, so if you can reuse anything in your interior that would normally be ripped out and thrown in a skip, do try. Aged textures and patina in your space are a huge plus. Seek out salvaged materials, such as parquet wooden floors or old wooden wall panelling. Reclaimed doors, such as this one at Ewelme Road in London, can add impact, and a salvaged mantelpiece can ground your space.

Composite Waste

The zero-waste movement is in full swing, taking discarded products that would otherwise end up in landfill and using them to make beautiful materials, from tabletops to tiles and splashbacks. The oldest form of this is probably the comeback-classic terrazzo – a traditional way to turn waste marble into something beautiful. New brand Alusid has taken this to the next level, making contemporary terrazzos and glazed tiles from TV screens and other electronic waste (above).

Linen and Hemp

As textiles go, linen and hemp are about as sustainable as they come. Produced from fast-growing plants that require less water than cotton to grow, they also happen to be really lovely. We use linen curtains all the time, such as in this bedroom for a project in Kew, London, and are looking into using hemp more and more. The latter can be used for rugs, carpets and accessories and waste is limited. Hemp is not as widely available as it should be for interiors, but the more demand we generate, the more products will appear on the market.

Vegan Alternatives

Veganism has become increasingly popular, not only because of its animal welfare benefits, but also for environmental reasons. We've been increasingly seeking out vegan alternatives for our designs and discovered Piñatex several years ago. It's an amazing alternative to leather that is made from pineapple leaves – a byproduct of the existing pineapple trade. We used it on the chair shown here. In fact, many leather alternatives are now available, including mushroom leathers and a range of faux leathers developed by international brand Ultrafabrics.

Dirk Vander Kooij

'My most beloved thing at home is a tie between Pip, my girlfriend, and an ingot of aluminium'

Experimental product designer Dirk Vander Kooij is a world leader when it comes to materiality. He was at the forefront of the recycled-plastic design movement (yes, that is a thing) and continues to push the boundaries of what is possible, taking humble waste material and turning it into things of beauty using extrusion and new 3D-printing techniques. We have one of his recycled-plastic vases in our home and it will always be treasured. We first met Dirk in Paris early in our interiors careers at Maison et Objet, the furniture and product fair, and have loved following his design journey.

My Interior Roadmap

My three materials are aluminium, plant cells and animal cells. My three key colours are green, black and beige and my three feelings at home are sleepy, tipsy and horny. My three functions are sleeping, drawing and cuddling.

What Home Means to Me

I live and work in the same building and my home environment wasn't important at all until quite recently. For so many years, my workshop was my home, and we're only now making a point to differentiate between these two spaces. The plants don't seem to mind the mess, so we're trying not to rush any big decisions. I share my home with my girlfriend, Pip, and a mouse. The mouse is tidy enough but Pip leaves crumbs and bits of shredded paper everywhere.

We're based on an old Dutch ammunitions manufacturing base about 5 km (3 miles) from the centre of Amsterdam. The terrain is made up of a collection of factories that were particularly active during the First and Second World Wars, although the whole lot has been abandoned for the last forty years or so. The building itself is a three-storey warehouse, with all sorts of funny angles and a sniper lookout on the roof. When I moved in four years ago, there were only dirt roads and broken widows – now they're talking about building high-rise apartments between the factories. We have a flooded basement level with collapsing beams and absolutely no natural light –it's honestly terrifying (once the water is pumped out it will make for an incredible lighting showroom). Another challenge with the space – I know this sounds incredibly petty – is there are too many windows. The upstairs apartment is a big open space lined entirely with windows. Our Vitamin D levels are fine, but our sock drawer is frustratingly nomadic.

My most beloved thing at home is a tie between Pip and an ingot of aluminium.

Relaxing and Entertaining

I like to relax at home in bed with a beer listening to either Action Bronson or John Mayer. If my home were a movie it would be somewhere between two – one realistic and one aspirational. The realistic movie is *Shrek* (2001), particularly his swamp; and the aspirational movie is Jaques Tati's *Mon Oncle* (1958). The latter places the traditional on the same plane as the ultra-modern, which is how we imagine the space when it's done. Our ideal number of guests would be two – Russell and Jordan.

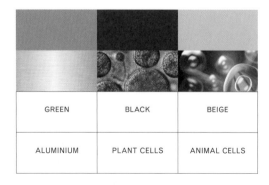

GREEN	BLACK	BEIGE
ALUMINIUM	PLANT CELLS	ANIMAL CELLS

ABOVE

Dirk's Fresnal pendant light and Melting Pot table are cutting-edge products made from humble waste materials.

RIGHT

Dirk uses bespoke colour options on products, including his Melting Pot table, to enhance their appeal.

Materiality: Feeling Space

Granville Park, London

This property was originally three flats and, working closely with our clients and their architect, we completely redesigned and renovated the layout to create five generous bedrooms and three en suite bathrooms. Home to three generations, the house also has a master bedroom suite (including a walk-in wardrobe) for Mum and Dad, an en suite bedroom for Grandma, and bedrooms and a bathroom for the children in the loft.

The project is packed full of clever storage solutions and exciting new materials with eco credentials, such as a bespoke recycled-plastic dining table. The use of recycled plastic continues into the kitchen, the master bathroom and the children's bathroom on the top floor, creating a throughline that takes you on a journey through the house.

To connect the home's bright, gallery-like spaces, we created a moment of compression at the entrance to the main living space with a richly coloured, curved ceiling tunnel. The bespoke geometric fabric we chose for a seat within the built-in shelving draws you though the 'tunnel', creating a focal point that connects the living and dining spaces. We designed the engineered wooden floor, with brass trim detail, to be laid geometrically in directions that vary depending on the functions of the different spaces. Specially commissioned wall murals provide a throughline of colour that leads to the children's rooms upstairs.

Three Colours
Blue, mint green, yellow

Three Materials
Valchromat (coloured fibreboard), recycled plastic, washed oak

Three Functions
Family space, disco, displaying art

Three Feelings
Inspired, creative, loved

Home Title
A Gallery of Life

OPPOSITE

This bespoke painted mural in one of the children's bedrooms was commissioned from artists Gilles & Cecilie and is brought to life with a glass balloon wall light.

ABOVE

The living space is like a gallery for everyday life, with neutral walls and joyful pieces that populate it with colour and pattern.

LEFT

The minimal impact of the kitchen is all about function, with fun found in the art, upholstery and furniture.

Materiality: Feeling Space

Railroaded (or grid-laid) tiles, concrete basins and a bespoke vanity made from recycled plastic sheet make this design special, and create a connection to the materials used elsewhere in the home.

Blue Valchromat cabinetry and a recycled-plastic dining table create the perfect setting for this artwork by Super Mundane, local to the family.

Materiality: Feeling Space

Unexpected Uses

Sometimes it's great to explore the unexpected. We have used materials in unusual ways in several of our design projects, but the decision always came from an authentic place and was born out of the desire to solve a problem space or to change the perception of a room.

An example would be tiling a whole chimney breast, which we did in our own kitchen and dining area (see page 102). Originally divided into two separate rooms, our new open-plan space ended up having two chimneys, but with no need for two fireplaces, we blocked the kitchen chimney breast and tiled it and its opening floor to ceiling. In fact, this is the only area in the kitchen that is tiled and its only function is to be beautiful. The small mosaic tiles are handmade and, although they were an extravagance, they do serve three spaces: the kitchen, the studio and the dining area.

Using materials in surprising ways can create a real talking point in a room – a moment of interest. Let your roadmap guide you so that you stay on track, but allow that path to take you to unexpected places.

Curtain Walls

Go big with your window treatments and don't restrict yourself to using curtains only for windows. We like to take curtains from floor to ceiling and from wall to wall, making windows feel bigger and adding softness to the structure of a room, as shown in this bedroom we designed in Islington, London. To create a snug that is next-level cosy, you could try curtaining all four walls with floor-to-ceiling velvet. We have also been known to add a curtain wall behind a bed, simply to add another dimension of texture.

Tiles Are Not Just for Bathrooms

This seems like a no-brainer – obviously you can use tiles in hallways, kitchens, fireplaces and elsewhere – but the idea of using tiles just for fun can be a mental block for some. Whether across a dining-room wall, such as in this project in Greenwich, London, or up a chimney breast, tiles can add interest, texture and colour and help to tie spaces together. Running tiles from a kitchen into the dining space, for example, can create connection between the two areas.

Chapter Five

Floors for Walls

You can add flow to a space by continuing wooden floorboards up a wall, or making a windowseat from your flooring material. In the design on the left, we used cork as a surface for the walls in order to create texture. Use materials to make connections and break conventions.

Mirror as Material

A mirror is not just for checking yourself out in. An incredibly useful material for shaping perceptions of space, light and depth, mirror can be used in many forms to create drama, give the illusion of more space and reveal reflections of key pieces.

Glass can be pricey, but get it cut to order by a local specialist and it is easy to install. Go big and try using interesting shapes and colours. We used a gold mirror for this island surface in our Brockley project (see page 146)

Rugs as Art

Beautiful rugs are an especially useful way to enhance your space if you are renting. Rugs can even be art for your walls – tapestries and wall hangings have been used for centuries. Rugs on walls add colour, pattern and texture, making a surprise contrast to more conventional framed prints and mirrors. They also dull sound, helping to create an instantly more relaxed atmosphere. We used a rug with a traditional pattern as a wall hanging in our Greenwich project.

Architectural
Lighting

Later we will look at the importance of designing your space
to work with natural light (see page 144). Now let's look at
architectural lighting – a way to manipulate light in your
home to create different moods and atmospheres.

Architectural lighting can massively affect the 'feel' of
your space. In the early stages of planning your design, it helps
to think about using light as a kind of material to wash across
a wall, define an area or highlight a focal point. While you are
thinking about walls, flooring and joinery materials, incorporate
any built-in lighting ideas you may have, from recessed spotlights
and wall lights to strip lights that highlight an entrance or special
feature. At this first stage, we are not talking about decorative
lighting (think lamps and pendants) – that will come later
on in the next chapter (page 142).

Spotlights

These have become overused in many homes, so we urge you to proceed with care. Spotlights can be good for functional areas, such as kitchens and bathrooms, but are not the only option. You can either opt for directional spotlights (like those in our Waterloo project below – see also page 120) or plastered-in versions that have no rim and give a seamless appearance. Always set spotlights on a separate switch to the other lighting in your space, so you can create different ambiences.

Functional Lights

We're talking about discreet lighting (like that shown below) in joinery, hidden in shelves, stairs, on landings and anywhere else where it provides a specifc function. This type of lighting is usually the remit of your architect, if you have one, but if not, it is worth taking time to think about how you might use these lights to elevate the function of your space. You could also try lighting that is triggered by motion sensors or opening doors – installation isn't as complex as you might think.

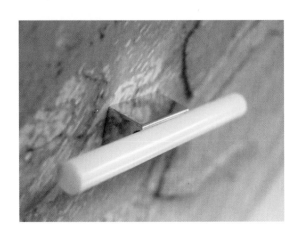

Wall Lights and Uplights

You may want to use these to highlight an artwork or light up a vaulted ceiling, but they can also be used to bring a level of ambient light to a room that is more about atmosphere than function, such as the one above from our home. Once out of favour, uplights are now on the rise and with good reason. They are a great way to create cosiness in a living room or snug.

Strip Lights

We are not talking old-skool flickering strip lights that hurt your eyes. Modern lighting is now much more advanced, with LED options and many variations that create warm or cool light and different levels of brightness. Strip lights can be plastered flush into walls and even furniture to add a contemporary edge to any space, as shown above in our closet.

Waterloo, London

The brief here was to create an elegant space with lots of natural light and an 'Instagrammable' kitchen (the owner is a cookery author and design journalist), banishing the owner's past memories of the space to create a new environment for personal growth. A complete renovation was needed, with a bold new internal layout; several walls were removed to create an open-plan living–dining–kitchen space. Our design included a calming bedroom with a pocket door, built-in storage made from Valchromat (a through-coloured particle board) and a luxurious wall upholstered in grey velvet behind the bed.

The building itself, a Brutalist concrete apartment block, also had a big influence on our design. We softened its grey concrete with sage greens, natural marble and linen to add a level of elegance and reference the homeowner's love of nature and cooking. Brutalism also gets a nod with our use of cast-aluminium lighting throughout, which grounds the interior in its architectural setting. A floor-to-ceiling curtain wall connects the living and dining areas, softening the space and making the small living-room window seem much larger.

The journey through this home feels defined and zoned, with each part of the property having its own atmosphere. We used one flooring material throughout to create flow. The modest size and limited colour palette of this project meant that materiality was key and we chose a wide variety of materials, including herringbone flooring, brass hardware and layers of textural fabrics, from modest broad-weave linen to deep-pile velvet. A wall of sliding mirrored doors, in smoked glass, bounces light into the dark hallway and gives the illusion of space. As a moment of extravagance that elevates the whole interior, we also designed a brass-clad opening between the entrance hall and the main living space. This idea came to us halfway through the project, as sometimes the best things do – it's important to be open to new ideas at every stage.

Three Colours
Pigeon grey, sage green, chalk

Three Materials
Smoked oak, brass, marble

Three Functions
Dine, cook, retreat

Three Feelings
Fresh, revitalized, safe

Home Title
Urban Luxe Micro Pad

OPPOSITE

The lighting scheme includes spotlights,
wall lights, lamps and this modest but beautiful
pendant light by British designer Dan Schofield.

ABOVE

This reading nook has a touch of Italian glamour,
with brass details and layers of luxurious velvet.

RIGHT

The use of brass continues into the bathroom,
juxtaposed with the concrete sink that feels perfect
for the Brutalist setting.

ABOVE

A brass-panelled door opens to reveal the
heavy curtained wall and herringbone floors that make
this space feel richly layered.

Chapter Five

Natural stone, mixed metals and neutral paintwork create
playful yet understated texture in the kitchen.

Materiality: Feeling Space

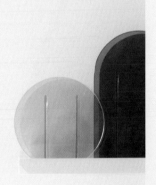

Chapter Six

Things:
The Stuff
of Life

This chapter is about all the things that would fall out if you held your home upside down.

Interiors are not just about having nice furniture and objects prettily arranged in a room. Your relationship with your possessions, their place in your home and the stories they tell are important.

Approach your things positively and with your roadmap in mind. Allow yourself to move on from objects you no longer need in order to surround yourself with possessions that strengthen your sense of self.

Choosing the right things for your interior will help you to create a better living environment, but never become obsessed by your purchases. Think of the possessions you bring into your home as characters in your story, each adding colour to your life. When you buy mindfully or collect with purpose, your things mean so much more.

The Weight of Things

Imagine a world where we are all creatures living in a wasteland, doomed to carry on our backs the weight of all the things we have bought or collected in our lives. You may recognize this from epic Jim Henson movie *Labyrinth* (1986; below) – a way-ahead-of-its-time fantasy dystopia.

Think about your things and feel the weight of them in your life. If the weight of them is easy to bear, or even makes you smile, then you are doing pretty well. For others, having too much stuff is the curse of modern life. If you are struggling under the weight of all your things, then it is time for a change, not only to what you own, but, more importantly, to your mindset. You need to let the right things into your life, so they don't weigh you down any more.

'Experiences, not things'

PAGE 124 AND OPPOSITE

Shelving can be brought to life with plants, favourite books and collected vases or other ceramics.

LEFT AND ABOVE

When all of the stuff in your life overwhelms you, it's time to get organized with some editing and curated displays.

Chapter Six

Three Types
of Things

Functional   This could be anything from the chair that you're sitting on to the vase of flowers on your table. Functional things have purpose and fulfil a need. These things are keepers.

Beautiful   There is always a little space for something purely beautiful in your home. In the words of John Keats, 'a thing of beauty is a joy forever'. You are the one who decides what you find beautiful, so only let things into your life that you love. If you can find things that are both beautiful and functional, you are winning.

Useless   If it's neither beautiful nor functional, we say get rid of it, or pass it on to someone else who would appreciate it. Head to sites such as eBay to sell your items or donate things you don't need to charity. Avoid landfill where possible and learn to choose your things more consciously to help you avoid buying more useless things in future.

Choosing the Right Things to Join You on Your Journey

The world is full of products vying for your attention, so how do you navigate through the mountain of tat to find the things that matter to you and make you smile, such as this dachshund we love? Now that your design is taking shape and you better understand your personal style, use this as your guide. Take your time when choosing a purchase, avoiding impulse buys. If this is a challenge at first, you could try assigning each item its own personal 'weight' (in terms of its value to you) and ask yourself whether you want to carry that weight with you on your journey.

Another good tip when you are shopping is to assess the difference between 'want' and 'need'. Ask yourself if it is a desire that will pass. If an item lingers in your thoughts and won't let you go, it may end up moving from the 'want' to the 'need' pile – sometimes the heart wins over the head.

'In a world full of brass pineapples and faux cacti...be a 3D-printed dachshund.'

Paul the Horse

We found this Royal Doulton white porcelain foal in a tiny vintage shop near where we live more than a decade ago and he has been with us ever since. We named him Paul – rather an incongruous name for such a delicate creature – and he is both elegant and comedic. We love him not just because of how delicate he is and his Royal Doulton heritage or the fact that we have a micro-obsession with horses in our home, but because of the large number of breaks he has suffered over the years by friends (and by us on one occasion). He has become symbolic of everything we have been through together and we couldn't love him more, yellowing glue stains and all. There is a modesty and honesty about Paul that makes us smile.

What are the objects in your life that will always have a home with you?

Shelley Simpson

'My home is where I have the time to muse on what is and plan what's next'

Known for clean lines and beautiful colours that work in any interior, the minimalist porcelain of Mud Australia, founded by Shelley Simpson, has become a global must-have. Shelley designs all the pieces herself and these are then made by hand in her Sydney studio, making this small business the perfect antidote to mass-produced ceramics. Mud Australia caught our attention many years ago for their striking simplicity and we love their relaxed approach to design. Here is an insight into the home of one very lovely, hands-on designer.

My Interior
Roadmap

I love concrete, brick and, of course, porcelain in my home (although I also love stainless steel and marble). My three colours are currently grey, blue and red, and the three feelings I associate with my home are comfortable, calm and collected. The three key functions of my living space are to nurture, restore and entertain.

What Home
Means to Me

My home is in the inner Sydney suburb of Newtown and I share it with my partner, James, and teenage son, Spencer. It's a four-storey heritage-listed 1860s terrace that we rebuilt a few years ago to reimagine its 19th-century proportions into our dream 21st-century home. With lots of generous private space throughout, it has a great shared kitchen/living room. We've retained original features and materials where we can, but all the functional rooms have been completely modernized.

Our architects worked with us to clearly define all the spaces in the home and their functions. We spent a lot of time thinking about interiors we admired and stole what we could. All the joinery, fittings, furnishings and materials have been chosen because of their form and function. The combined kitchen/living area was inspired by the kitchen in Donald Judd's SoHo studio and this is where we spend most of our time, although the bedroom suite is also a favourite – we lost another bedroom in the house to make ours bigger. You enter the room through the wardrobe and it's big enough to include a lounge, our en suite and access to a balcony in the trees and rooftops. It's extremely private and calm.

My most beloved things are my children, my partner and my Serge Mouille lamp, in no particular order. Having a four-storey home has become a little inconvenient post-hip replacement, but the house has a lot of stories to tell. When we were rebuilding it, we had two beautiful little cavoodles named Paris and Nikki (yes, after the Hilton sisters). As part of the building spec, we built them a secret tunnel from our courtyard into the kitchen pantry. Sadly, they've now gone to the crazy dog party in the sky, but their memory remains.

Relaxing
and Entertaining

My home is my sanctuary and inspiration. It's where I relax and connect with family and friends, but also where I have the time to muse on what is and plan what's next! Just before sleep is when I relax – this might involve an episode of TV shows *Escape to the Country* or *Grand Designs*, but otherwise I'll be pottering (apt for a potter). The music I listen to at home depends on who's around, but I like the Carpenters, Aretha Franklin, Ella Fitzgerald, Paul Kelly and BBC6. I'm obsessed with interiors in movies, too, so if my home were a movie, maybe it would be *I Am Love* (2009) – without the emotional baggage – or *Ex Machina* (2014) – we dream.

GREY	RED	BLUE
CONCRETE	BRICK	PORCELAIN

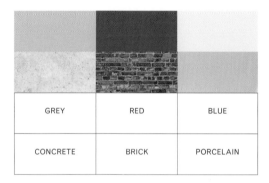

Mud Australia's delicate handmade
plates in soft green.

The inviting kitchen space in Shelley's home
from a shoot by Petrina Tinsley. With its open
displays, functional layout and warm wood, this
is a room ready for tea and a lovely chat.

New Things

When you bring something new into your home, not just new to you but newly made, you bring freshness and excitement with it. Whether a new piece of art to sit above your mantelpiece that won your heart, a laundry basket you watched the weaver make at a craft show, a vase that is perfectly designed to hold your favourite tulips or a linen cushion in blush pink to add impact to your sofa, if it puts a smile on your face and helps facilitate a better life for you, then grasp it with both hands and welcome it into your home. This holds true as long as your piece fits within the story you are creating for your interior. Remember not to fall back into the trap of micro-shopping and always be mindful of the new things you let in.

Commissioning something bespoke can cost slightly more than buying 'off the shelf', but will give back so much more. Getting to know the maker and helping them to grow their business can connect you to a thing in powerful ways. Bringing something truly personal into your life is one of the joys of the creative process.

Prized possessions on display in our living room: a hand-cast metal bowl by Kalsaff and Changing vase by Dirk Vander Kooij.

Chapter Six

Old Things

There is no room that will not benefit from an object with history. Things that have led a life and have stories to tell in their cracks or patina will ground your interior and give it life. Try to get the right balance of objects in your home that have different stories to tell from different time periods and your space will be infinitely more human.

Shopping vintage is good for the soul and a great way to hone your style. Search through until you happen upon a piece that grabs your heart and treat the process as a positive way to learn about what you like.

There are so many great pre-loved things in our world that could be just what you are looking for. We often trawl second-hand websites, such as eBay, looking for the perfect pieces for our projects. It's good to do this with an open mind and you may find a hidden gem. For example, if you're looking at upholstered chairs and sofas, always look at shapes as well as fabrics. It can sometime be hard to see past an ugly pattern but, if you love it otherwise, consider getting it reupholstered.

Let us not forget that buying vintage and reusing someone else's unwanted items is also good for the planet. We have already used up so many natural resources and if we learn to cherish our things more, perhaps we will also become more mindful about how we choose to make our things in the future.

<u>ABOVE</u>

Bringing a client's inherited furniture out of storage and back into use helped us create this gorgeous writing corner.

Curating Your Things

Express yourself and don't hide away in a cupboard.
Remember our house-shy character from earlier on? Your home
is your space, so banish embarrassment and get out that artwork
you did, display that unique collection of 80s memorabilia and
shout about that selection of rare succulents that you've nurtured.
It doesn't matter what your passion is, there is a way to display it
creatively that will represent you in the best way.

Make sure your home has wall space and shelf space to
put your things on display, and keep that display alive by adding
and editing as you go. Think of your home as an art gallery that
embodies your life, with you as the curator. Your life's expression
could be a display on a shelf or mantelpiece or even just changing
up the scatter cushions on your sofa.

Everything in its Place

Having a special place to put your things elevates their
importance and helps you both to appreciate what you have
and to make better choices about new items. Do you really want
that new piece to become part of your collection? Whether it
be a shelf, sideboard or storage unit, give your things a place
and store them there. We said store, not hide. The trick is to
rotate your pieces so that you don't feel overwhelmed or bored
by your stuff. If you have a place to keep some of your beloved
objects safe, you can bring them out and rotate them to bring
a fresh approach to your things every so often.

Break the Symmetry

Think about creating visual interplay with your pieces. For
example, try using different heights and scales to create an
appealing display of vases on a sideboard. You could also try
grouping by colour or material, which can work beautifully. Try
to stick to odd numbers of items in your groups and break up
symmetry to add life and interest (symmetrical displays rarely
work unless you are in a stately home or going for a grand feel).

OPPOSITE

Containing your things in one shelving area allows you to mix lots of elements up within a defined space.

ABOVE

Slimline picture shelves can offer a great changeable display space for art, photos and books.

Creating a Shelfie, Not Just a Cliché

The word 'shelfie' is undeniably overused, but it's a cliché for good reason. Editing is as important as creating.

Make a shelfie to unlock connections between your items, curating the pieces that you love in a meaningful way.

We like to change our shelfies at home all the time. We have cupboards full of vases and objects that we love and we rotate them almost seasonally. There are no rules here, so just display what you love. We try to layer artworks with vases and even books that inspire us, then we add plants. Play, don't be afraid of getting it wrong, and keep it simple!

Integrating Vintage

Hand-me-downs and flea-market finds can be wonderfully grounding, softening the edge of a new interior and bedding it in. Use vintage pieces in the right way and you can create moments of real wonder in your home. Whether contrasted with clean modern elements, curated en masse, or repurposed and reimagined, build them into your design. Here are three examples of how we have used vintage pieces in our projects.

Vintage Wardrobe Doors (left)

The patina of these reclaimed exterior doors, repurposed into doors for a bespoke wardrobe, bring life to this pared-back bedroom, with its bare plaster walls. A functional solution for hiding the closet space, the doors also add a layer of colour and texture to the room.

Using vintage pieces is not always about just shopping and placing, sometimes it takes some imagination – and the help of a skilled joiner – to see how a piece can be best used in your space.

Revamped Vanity Cabinet (opposite)

We love vintage pieces – they give an instant lived-in feeling that you just can't achieve with an entirely new scheme – but they can need a little love and customization to work in your space. In this project, we found the perfect Victorian chest of drawers and turned it into a double vanity cabinet for this master bathroom by restoring its zinc top and sawing a little off the legs to alter its height.

ABOVE

The softness of bare plaster creates a beautiful layer in this bedroom, with the bed's bold headboard and selection of vibrant cushions.

LEFT

A hallway is a wonderful place for bold pattern, as it is a transient space.

OPPOSITE

We painted the original cast-iron fire surround to match the wall colour, bedding it into the architecture of the room to let the owners' possessions sing.

Ver Road, Hertfordshire

Originally a modest semi-detached cottage in a charming countryside setting, this house was in need of modernization throughout. We redesigned the entire property, adding extensions to the kitchen, first floor and loft to double the size of the home and create a characterful family living space. We added striking reclaimed blue pillars between the new kitchen extension and the older part of the house to create an incredible link between these two spaces.

This happy home has a throughline of bold colour and pattern – a signature of ours – that brings it to life. The vintage pieces throughout create a relaxed vibe that gives a nod to a love of travel and the sea. Bespoke encaustic tiles in unique colourways, natural-edged wooden worktops and a marbled-concrete kitchen island add material joy. Classic Liberty print florals for the wallpaper and carpet situate the home in the Edwardian period and its natural setting.

Three Colours
Pink, pale grey, teal

Three Materials
Gloss tiles, washed oak, concrete

Three Functions
Relax, entertain, play

Three Feelings
Safe, unique, love

Home Title
Rock 'n' Roll Eclectic Cottage

Reclaimed architectural pillars, with their original
paintwork intact, frame the new extension beautifully and
connect it to the period features of the home.

Colour and pattern bring this new kitchen extension
to life, with open shelving and a vintage trolley to show
off useful and beautiful things.

Things: The Stuff of Life

Home Jewelry:
Lamps and Pendants

We've already covered architectural lighting on
page 118: now it's time to look at more decorative lighting
options – the jewelry of the home, if you will. Think of your lamps
and pendants as accessories. Of course, all lighting should be
functional – that goes without saying – but it should also
be beautiful, playful and impactful, much like a carefully
chosen pair of earrings or an eyecatching necklace.

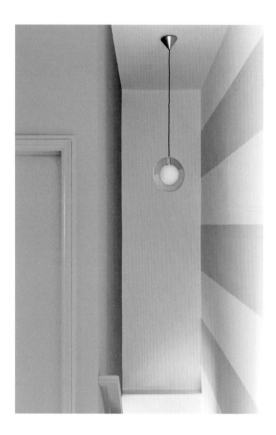

Pendants

Use these to create drama in the middle of a room or bring
atmosphere to a specific zone, such as above a dining table
or kitchen island or at the centre of a living space or bedroom.
You can even opt for pendants as bedside lighting to leave your
bedside table free of lamps. Plan the location of your pendants
well in advance for easier installation. If you are at a late stage
in your project, you can try plug-in pendants or use a ceiling
hook to move the position of a light to where it's most needed.

A stairway can be the perfect place for a decorative lighting
moment. In the project on the left, we used a small pendant
light with big impact. The powerful shape makes a great
material statement, with its brass finish against the colourful
stripes painted on the walls.

Lamps

Whether of the table, desk or floor variety, these beauties are
not to be forgotten. They can offer task lighting, for reading or
working, but they can also create ambience. What room doesn't
look gorgeous by lamplight, especially if you are looking to
generate a relaxed vibe? A table lamp, such as the one opposite
from our home, can provide an atmospheric diffused light. This
classic downward-facing design also prevents bulb glare.

Bringing the Light in

Here's where we tie together those disparate elements
of electrical joy, breaking our lighting obsession down into
layers that you can play with. This is not a lighting manual, but a
way of thinking about light as you plan your project. First identify the
best-lit areas, the challenging spaces and the functions you need your
lighting to perform. Then think about what type of light will work
best for the space, whether architectural or decorative. And
finally, go back to your roadmap to tie that lighting in to the
colours and materials you have chosen to work with.

→

Natural Light
Where do your spaces benefit the most
from natural light over the course of the
day? Think about placing your room's key
areas in these spaces, leaving the rest
down to electricity to add beauty and
create atmosphere. We placed the
dining area in our Ewelme Road project
in order to get the most from the
natural light in the space.

Chapter Six

↑

Architectural Lighting – As we discussed earlier, this is the type of lighting – spotlights, wall lights, recessed lighting – that benefits from a bit of forward planning, so start early. Think of this as creating general washes of light that allow a space to be functional.

↑

Decorative Lighting – Vintage or modern, big or small, brash or humble, lamps and pendants come in many styles. Have fun with them.

Task Lighting – Who doesn't love a lamp for working and other practical tasks at home? Invest in design classics and you can take them with you wherever you make a home.

Statement Lighting – Think of this type of light as 'the one', the budget buster or reclaimed special find, such as this pendant from our Brockley project (see overleaf). Use it to service open-plan spaces or create grand moments. Statements should be used sparingly, but when you do, go for it.

Brockley, London

The challenge with this project was to take a shell of a Victorian townhouse and make it into a modern space that reflected the different styles of the lovely couple who live there. The colour palette modulates to create different atmospheres, making the spaces a fine balance between total opulence and the rawness of honest materials, including concrete, brass and steel. We had a lot of fun with the lighting in particular, combining statement pieces with vintage and bespoke furniture to create a dramatic 'curated' feel that flows throughout. We also designed custom joinery for several of the spaces, which makes this home feel truly unique.

Three Colours
Blue, stone, deep rose

Three Materials
Brass, smoked oak, concrete

Three Functions
Entertain, relax, celebrate

Three Feelings
Chic, grown-up, unique

Home Title
Humble Luxe Magic

OPPOSITE

When a lamp becomes sculpture,
by Michael Anastassiades for Flos.

LEFT

This delicate bubble pendant by Giopato & Coombes
is an elegant touch that elevates the bathroom space.

BELOW

We used pendant lights in place of bedside table
lamps to free up the bedside surfaces.

These plaster wall lights can be painted to match the wall colour, receding when not in use and creating ambience when turned on.

When a wall light becomes art: beautiful on or off.

Things: The Stuff of Life

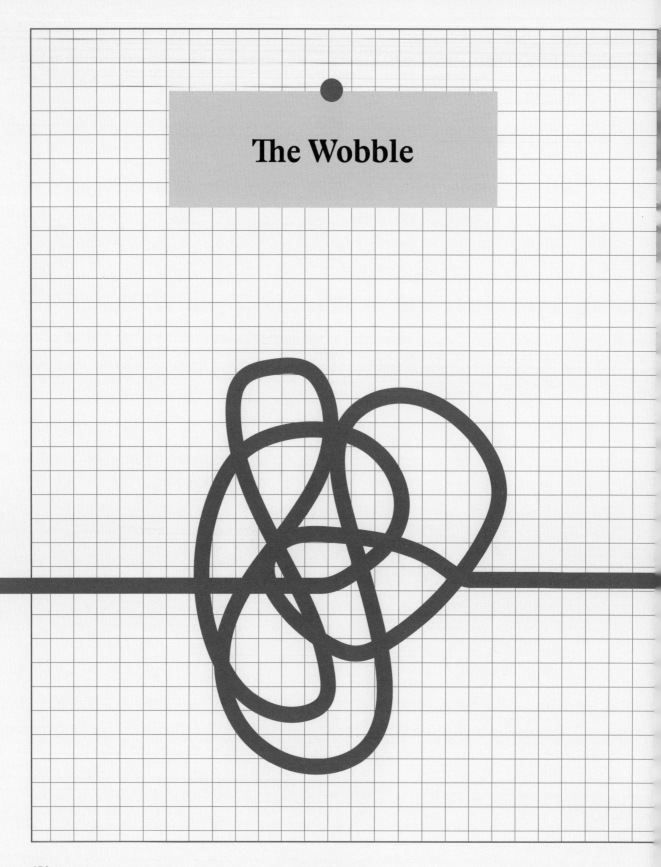

The Wobble

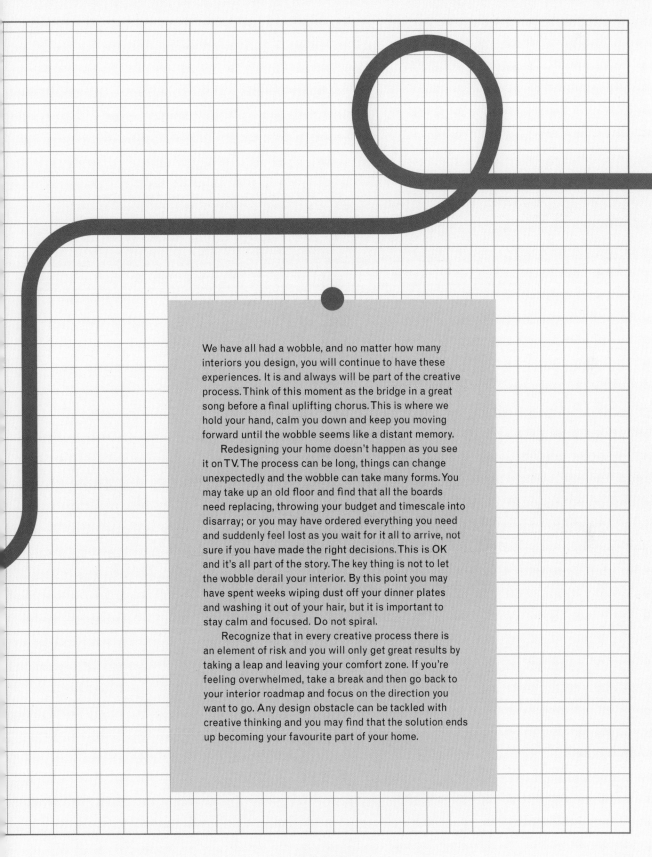

We have all had a wobble, and no matter how many interiors you design, you will continue to have these experiences. It is and always will be part of the creative process. Think of this moment as the bridge in a great song before a final uplifting chorus. This is where we hold your hand, calm you down and keep you moving forward until the wobble seems like a distant memory.

Redesigning your home doesn't happen as you see it on TV. The process can be long, things can change unexpectedly and the wobble can take many forms. You may take up an old floor and find that all the boards need replacing, throwing your budget and timescale into disarray; or you may have ordered everything you need and suddenly feel lost as you wait for it all to arrive, not sure if you have made the right decisions. This is OK and it's all part of the story. The key thing is not to let the wobble derail your interior. By this point you may have spent weeks wiping dust off your dinner plates and washing it out of your hair, but it is important to stay calm and focused. Do not spiral.

Recognize that in every creative process there is an element of risk and you will only get great results by taking a leap and leaving your comfort zone. If you're feeling overwhelmed, take a break and then go back to your interior roadmap and focus on the direction you want to go. Any design obstacle can be tackled with creative thinking and you may find that the solution ends up becoming your favourite part of your home.

Chapter Seven

Joyful
Minimalism

This chapter is where you bring everything together – clean lines, focused function, colour, pattern, materials and pretty things to flesh out your space in your personal style. Just like gender, sexuality and creativity, your style is on a scale. None of us fit into perfect boxes and these complexities are what make each of us unique. We each have different combinations of experiences and traits that result in our personal styles.

Our own style has taken years to develop and we call it Joyful Minimalism. It's a new take on living in your home that combines the best of both worlds: a minimalist approach to line and function, and a joyful approach to colour, pattern and shape. Creative freedom is at the heart of our approach and we want to share our ideas with you to help you discover your own personal style.

Minimalist Mind
Maximalist Heart

Now you've got further in the process of designing your home, you may find yourself pulled in two distinct design directions, trapped into indecision because you can't decide what bracket your style falls into. The thing is, you don't have to decide. Different ideas can exist in the same space. We believe in a non-binary world and we want you to have that freedom. It's fine to be one extreme one day and the opposite extreme the next, or somewhere in the middle all the time.

Allow yourself the freedom of not defining your style. Choosing a home title (see page 29) should help you to crystallize your direction for a project in a more abstract way that defies definition. Never get trapped in a box. Be true to yourself in your style and modulate your ideas accordingly. A home can be as complex as you and as simple as you need it to be. Let it be free.

PAGE 152

The painted stairs and terrazzo floor we designed for Crown Paints show how much can be achieved with simple means.

ABOVE, LEFT AND RIGHT

Pared-back styling with key colours, versus powerful maximal wallpaper and styling, both in our Kew Penthouse project.

'Think of your style on a scale: it never has to be either/or. It can be levels of lots of different things.'

Living in a
Digital World

The digital age has made every style throughout history easily accessible and allows us to share looks in a global melting pot, all at our fingertips. We can happily borrow a bit of Bauhaus spirit and blend it with some Baroque principles, mix Victoriana with a little Bloomsbury Group, or create an industrial edge with a minimal touch. We can cross oceans and bring global cultures together in our choice of colours, materials and styles, mixing Mediterranean hues with American coastal or Japanese principles with Scandinavian function. We can even cross space and take an intergalactic approach, with the likes of retro and modern futurism, conceptual interiors from Mars and spaceship chic. Whatever floats your boat, OK?

For our online personas, interiors stand and fall on the likes they get and the shares they receive. The danger here is that individuality and authenticity get lost in the bargain.

Even subconsciously, you may design your home based partly on the most popular trends, and this can affect us all. Even as you try to create something for yourself, you can't help but be influenced, and so interiors start to look homogenous.

Much as social media has democratized interior design, it has also facilitated a blanket approach, which, in turn, has an effect on how and what big brands choose to market to us – and design begins to consume itself. We once got invited to an influencer event, hosted by one of the big social platforms, where all the spaces were designed using the data of their users. The influencers were there to get inspired by things they had most likely had a hand in designing, indirectly or not. In this way, 'inspirations' can become second- or even third- or fourth-hand until every design is singing from the same hymn sheet.

Interior Tribes

We love to look at both sides of any situation, as a couple with very different approaches, and despite design styles becoming increasingly homogenous, you can also argue that interior tribes are becoming more and more distinct. Team grey became team pink and it's easy to spot the 'ban the beige' brigade, the bold interiors movement, Scandi diehards, Brutalist hipsters, the luxury interiors club, dedicated Deco lovers, minimalists and maximalists, upcyclers and crafters, naturalists, futurists and Eurotrash modernists. There's nothing wrong with any of this. We all love to get behind something and make an easy-to-love statement about who we are. The danger, though, if you subscribe too hard, is that you remove your sense of self from the equation. If you aren't careful, interior tribes are boxes that you can become trapped inside.

It's better to enjoy multiple tribes, respecting them all, so that you can embrace elements of each and mix up your own style. Just like a cocktail, an interior doesn't work if it is all one flavour. It only comes to life when you combine multiple ingredients, such as fizz, fruit, spices and florals. Throw in a twist of lime and a spritz of new-wave soda and you can have it all.

Uniqueness

Interior gurus and their tribes have been worshipping at this fountain for so long and their mantra of 'here's how to make your home unique' has spread across the globe.

The truth is, aiming for uniqueness is nonsense. It is not something to be achieved, it merely is. You couldn't fail to be unique if you tried. So stop focusing on it as a marker of success. Accept that who you are, the home you live in, the moment in time you find yourself in, where you are and where you have been will always make a unique combo.

The gauge of what is unique and what isn't is usually based on comparison to others. How do you know something is unique? Just because no one else is doing it? This is bull. We established earlier that comparison is the death of creativity and so the race to be unique is a fool's game. Take it away and you can enjoy who you are – a natural one-off – rather than comparing any part of yourself to others. In doing so, you can create a home that reflects the very best of your authentic self.

Chapter Seven

'Don't try to be unique. You don't need to try, because you already are and always will be.'

Finding Your Style

Whole books have been written about design movements, but it is enough for now to get an overview of the iconic styles that have shaped our homes today. Use this crib sheet to help you discover where you want to go. You don't have to choose a single style to follow – cherry-pick the bits you love and put them together into a wonderful new style that is all your own.

Italian Deco – This is about marble, brass, rich colours and luxury, all with an edge of Art Deco glamour. The Italian scene has always been a strong presence in the design world, with the annual Milan design festival leading the world. Recent years have seen a revival of all things 70s Deco, with curves, metallics and drama in excess, but did this influence ever really disappear? It's a lasting style that we keep coming back to in our designs.

↓

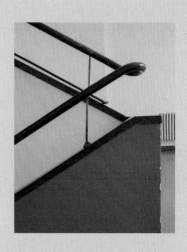

↑

Bauhaus – For many, this style is the origin of modern design. Founded by Walter Gropius in the early 20th century, Bauhaus was a school of design with colour and function at its foundation. Responsible for many of the iconic design classics we know and love, it has had a huge influence on modern design, graphics and architecture.

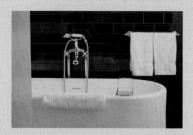

↑

Minimalism – The image of an empty white space comes to mind, but there is so much more to this movement. It's characterized by clean lines, limited palettes and bright open spaces, and is a way of life as much as a design movement. It emerged after World War II and also encompasses art, music, food and fashion. To live minimally is to do so with purpose and focus.

Midcentury Modern – The love for this retro movement never seems to wane. It's all about a passion for classic design and seeking out new and old pieces at fairs, festivals and online. From 50s kitsch to 60s chic, 70s glam and 80s cool, who doesn't have a piece of midcentury design in their home? It is a movement that covers so much and yet feels so defined, by its loyal following as much as anything.

→

Chapter Seven

Maximalism – This is the 'more is more' approach to design – think Hollywood regency, Dorothy Draper or William Morris. It's all about wallpapers, borders and trim brands, with layers upon layers of pattern and colour. This is a style that isn't bound to a specific era, but crops up again and again throughout design history. It has been attributed to the postmodern movement (a reaction against minimalism), but you could just as well trace it to the excesses of great monarchs, with their luxurious country manors and palaces, such as Versailles.

↓

Memphis – An anarchic design movement led by the visionary Ettore Sottsass that is influencing much of the current design scene. Founded in Milan in 1981, this movement gave us new ways of looking at colours and materials, playing with unexpected elements in bold, graphic ways to subvert the norm and expand our minds. It's brash but undeniably iconic.

↓

↑

Scandi – A cornerstone of interior design, Scandinavian style has infused itself into all areas of the design world, making homes cosier and more functional. This is a style in tune with nature, often featuring wood, natural textiles and flower and plant motifs. Placing high value on home, living standards and interior design, Scandinavians know how to live.

↑

Modern Craft – In our post-industrial age, we are looking to craft to aid our comfort and well-being. This is all about the mark of the maker and the hand of the designer. It is a return to the most primal of human skills, bringing form to clay or wood, weaving and working metal. A natural reaction to the disconnects of modern life, the modern craft movement represents a desire to return to a simpler time.

Biophilia – Living with plants is all about surrounding yourself with all that is green, to clean the air you breathe and create a sense of well-being. Architects and designers around the world are seeking to build a better world by living alongside nature rather than destroying it, and social media has helped reinvent houseplants as the chicest of home companions.

↓

Futurism – This is a style about the desire to reach forward and see what we could be and how we could live. It's all about innovative materials, new technologies, such as 3D printing, and recycled waste. Each era has had its futurists who look to subvert accepted ideas to find new and better ways to get the most from the spaces we have and the materials we use. Now, when we look back on futures past, they can seem like science fiction, with some ideas more successful than others, but we could all benefit from a little forward thinking to teach us better ways to live.

↓

Get Your Curve On

So many of the spaces we inhabit are angular,
with strong lines and hard edges, so every now and then,
allow yourself to break it up. Curves are the ultimate rule
breakers, offering a touch of the unexpected and bringing
organic shapes into your home. With roots in the Art Deco
era, curved shapes are a classic that keeps coming back,
so don't be afraid that they are a passing fancy. If you have
embraced the idea of thinking outside the box with your
design, they are a great way to push the boundaries.
From chairs and lights to beds and even kitchen
units, bring on the curves.

ABOVE

We designed our Luca bed, with its simple playful curves,
for Love Your Home.

Rise Up
The Rise Kitchen

Our house was candy pink when we bought it, with deep green carpets. This was one of the things that made us fall for it and we wanted to retain this inspiration in our redesign of the kitchen, while also being playful with contemporary shapes and colours. Half of our house still had its original 19th-century features and the other half had been renovated in the late 1950s, which gives the interior a lovely tension between two time periods. We tried to honour the heritage of the house in our kitchen design, using shades of pink and green in the colour scheme and restoring the fireplace and plasterwork. We then let ourselves play with different design styles to create our unique interpretation. We designed curved cabinets, lighting and a patterned table to help tie the space together in our own way.

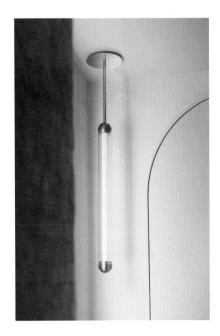

ABOVE

The kitchen design celebrates the original features, with our own playful additions, including lighting.

BELOW, LEFT AND RIGHT

Matching curved cabinets for the kitchen area.

Playfulness

Earlier we encouraged you to play within the lines, but now we want you to fully embrace the playful approach. The nirvana of interiors is a design that has taken time, thought and planning, but manages to feel fun and relaxed at the same time – a serious design that doesn't take itself too seriously. If you have followed the earlier chapters about understanding the structure of your space, you can now begin to add a little rebellion in the way you choose to disrupt that structure. Every room will benefit from some playfulness, showing you really know how to be free and you're not afraid to reflect that in your home.

Clash

Clashing colours is fun. As you grow in confidence on your home journey, throw colour theories out of the window. Use your three roadmap colours as a base and play by adding touches of other colours to mix it up. You can also try mixing metals and wood tones to add depth to the three materials of your roadmap. Sometimes through experiment, you will hit on an unconventional colour combo. Your head says, 'Move away from the table and put those colours back where they belong' – but your heart says, 'Why do I find it so dreamy?' Go with it.

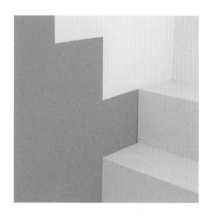

Play

Playing with scale is also a great way to free up a scheme that could be in danger of getting a little too serious. This might be a huge vintage chandelier that has no business being in a small bedroom or an enormous circular mirror above a small chair where you can tie your shoes in an entrance hallway. Often overlooked, scale can be lots of fun, so don't be afraid to go really big or really small. Power it up and be free with the size of your imagination.

Chapter Seven

'Take design seriously, but don't take yourself seriously.'

Disrupt

Once you have mastered the basics, it's fun to start disrupting the architecture of your home by juxtaposing different periods of design or by experimenting with shapes and lines that break the mould. If the physical bones are strong and the lines are clean as clean can be, then one element of madness will not hurt anyone. Whether a strip light in a period setting or a painted mural that breaks the lines of your doorframes (see page 164), this can be a decorative layer on top of the basic structure of your space that does not damage the design you have created, just plays with it, consciously.

Laugh

Allow a moment of wit in your interior, poking fun at yourself or challenging your guests with a naughty moment. Show no fear, but don't force it – nothing witty is ever forced. Showing you are able to laugh at yourself in your space will present a relaxed edge to who you are and how you choose to live, so don't edit out that comedy. Punctuate your interior with a cheeky twinkle in the eye.

Lipstick for Doors

This is the gateway to a joyful kitchen. Here we let you into our process and show you how we brought bold decorative curves into our space with paint and courage.

We took inspiration from the handprinted murals and decorative interior detailing of the Bloomsbury Group and from Ettore Sottsass, founder of the iconic Memphis movement. Both design approaches were born out of a desire to disrupt the norms with creativity and this is what we wanted to do in our space. The pink also feels right in our home as our hallway was painted this colour when we first bought the house. How vibrant is that colour? We couldn't resist – the pink told us what it wanted us to do with it, so we did. Here is how.

Chapter Seven

1

An illustration on paper is a great starting point to help you decide the shape and number of curves.

Count the scallops and scale it up for the real door. Divide the door measurements by the number of scallops you want.

2

Mark the high and low points with a pencil. We went for 30 cm (12 in.) for each full curve, so we marked the frame at 15 cm (6 in.) intervals.

4

Join the dots. The handpainted quality is what makes it special, so don't be a perfectionist, and let it be organic. Fill in the outlines, just like lipstick for your doorways.

3

Next dot the paint where you want the high and low points of the wave at 15 cm (6 in.) intervals. The dots for the high points should be around 10 cm (4 in.) from the frame.

Joyful Minimalism

Form Doesn't Always
Have to Follow Function

The home rebel will throw caution to the wind and choose sculptural shapes that are there 'just because', not necessarily always for the sake of function. Curves are a great example (see page 160). Not the most sensible of shapes for the spaces we live in, but fun and pleasing to the eye nonetheless.

Design rebels have been indulging in quirky shapes for many years. They show wit and a little bit of anarchy that lets all who enter your home see that you know how to have fun. Take the example of the red lips sofa, inspired by Salvador Dalí's Surrealist portrait of Mae West. The Design Museum

says of it: 'Initially a small production company responsible for the most iconic pieces of Italian radical design, Gufram became famous for merging art and design. Studio 65's Bocca sofa became one of its best-known pieces. The sofa's red colour is a Gufram exclusive, and its two corners are not perfectly symmetrical, just as human lips would be.'

When is a sofa not a sofa? When it is also a pair of lips, because you can. This is on the boundary of art and design and there is room for a flavour of this in the more rebellious home.

ABOVE

The legendary Bocca sofa by Studio 65 for Gufram (1972) at the 'Home Futures' exhibition at London's Design Museum.

Chapter Seven

Sometimes You Have to Go There to Come Back

With interiors, simplicity takes time, ideas are developed with friends and editing is key. Why is it that so often you end up buying the first thing you see even though you have been 'around the houses' and seen a maddening myriad of options? Well, sometimes you have to go there to come back. We say this often. The creative process can be instinctive, but analysis and research are also key to making good decisions. In order to be happy in the knowledge you have found the right sofa or the right material, you may follow a gut reaction in the first instance, but you also need to discover what else is out there in order to make sure your choice is the right one.

Keeping the idea that 'sometimes you have to go there to come back' in mind as you make choices will help to make the myriad of options you try far less maddening. Just because an initial idea fizzles out, or you find that a material you want to use is unsuitable for a job, it doesn't mean that the time spent was wasted. It is always beneficial to play and try out different ideas and you may just find that by digging deeper you unearth something new and wonderful.

Our training as actors is a big help when it come to making design decisions. Everything is valid in the rehearsal room – there's no wrong move, no wrong instinct. To try is to learn, so never allow fear or embarrassment to stop you. We often get asked where our creativity comes from and it is not a magic spark, it is a sense of freedom to try and to challenge each other's ideas openly, without judgment. Dare to explore.

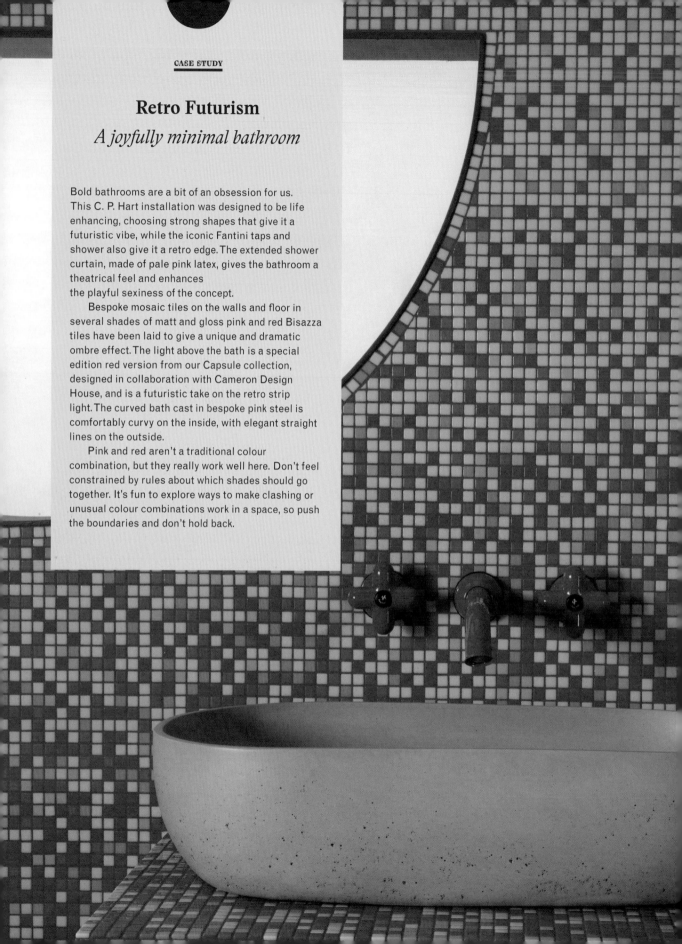

Retro Futurism

A joyfully minimal bathroom

Bold bathrooms are a bit of an obsession for us. This C. P. Hart installation was designed to be life enhancing, choosing strong shapes that give it a futuristic vibe, while the iconic Fantini taps and shower also give it a retro edge. The extended shower curtain, made of pale pink latex, gives the bathroom a theatrical feel and enhances the playful sexiness of the concept.

Bespoke mosaic tiles on the walls and floor in several shades of matt and gloss pink and red Bisazza tiles have been laid to give a unique and dramatic ombre effect. The light above the bath is a special edition red version from our Capsule collection, designed in collaboration with Cameron Design House, and is a futuristic take on the retro strip light. The curved bath cast in bespoke pink steel is comfortably curvy on the inside, with elegant straight lines on the outside.

Pink and red aren't a traditional colour combination, but they really work well here. Don't feel constrained by rules about which shades should go together. It's fun to explore ways to make clashing or unusual colour combinations work in a space, so push the boundaries and don't hold back.

CLOCKWISE FROM OPPOSITE

Pink sink by Kast; retro red taps by Fantini; classic mosaic tiles by Bisazza; bath with clean lines by Bette.

Joyful Minimalism

India Mahdavi

'Happy, happy, happy'

The world's best interiors speak for themselves and this is true of those by Parisian interior designer India Madhavi, whose design for the Sketch dining room in London is one of the most photographed of modern times. Always chic and full of joy, her impactful work has changed the way we see interiors forever. Describing her work as 'a cross-cultured art de vivre', Madhavi's designs reveal that less is more in the most wonderful way.

My Interior Roadmap

My three materials are ceramic, velvet and wood. Key colours are yellow, pink and green; and key functions are eat, sleep and dream. The three feelings I want my home to evoke are happy, happy, happy.

What Home Means to Me

My home in Paris, which I share with my son, has a sky view and is in a 17th-century U-shaped building, overlooking a central garden. The building has endless corridors, which is my least favourite aspect of my home, but I have too many favourite parts to mention. My most beloved things are my Chester drawings by Ettore Sottsass, founder of the Memphis design movement.

Relaxing and Entertaining

I like to relax by reading in front of the fireplace or listening to Miles Davis's *Kind of Blue*. For me, eight is the perfect number of guests for a dinner party, and if my home were a movie it would be *The Party* (1968) directed by Blake Edwards.

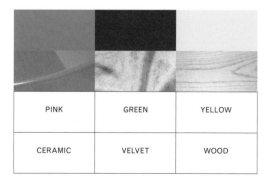

PINK	GREEN	YELLOW
CERAMIC	VELVET	WOOD

RIGHT

The Don Giovanni lamp, Charlotte chair and Bishop stool by India.

BELOW

This rug was designed by India as part of the Jardin Interieur collection for Cogolin, 'freeing the borders of a carpet to create infinite gardens at home'.

OVERLEAF

'Chez Nina', designed by India for Nilufar Gallery.

Joyful Minimalism

Chapter Seven

Joyful Minimalism

The Evolving Home: It's Alive!

If you have created an environment that allows you to live your best life, then you are winning, but life goes on, after all, and change is the one thing you can be certain of.

This chapter is about the importance of letting your home evolve. An interior is never finished – it's as alive as you are – so don't aim for perfection or the 'final reveal'. Create a space that makes you happy and let it grow with you. We change as people all the time, so it's fine to want to mix things up in your interior, too. The key is to tune in to what it is you love and need – the more you pay attention to your creative instincts, the louder they will shout. They are what will help you stay on track in the face of the continual distractions that trends, fads and daily life can throw at you.

Lovely is Forever

Leave room for life to happen in your space and you
will never feel the FOMO again. Your home should facilitate and
inspire you, rejuvenating your spirit as well as your body.
If you follow the tools in this book, and trust your own instincts
about colour and texture, you will have created a home that is as
adaptable and as right for you as your daily wardrobe.

Stop trying to get your home 'just right'. Once you've
nailed the essentials in each room, enjoy taking the time to
express yourself with ornaments, art and cushions – the jewelry
that brightens your day. You don't need to run to IKEA and buy
everything all at once while you wait for the paint on the
walls to dry. Enjoy the process of nurturing your home
and it will nurture you right back.

Everything for a Reason

Make conscious decisions that feel right for you and your
home to stop you falling back into the bad habit of mindless
purchasing.

Considered choices are all about taking the time to
understand and engage with your surroundings. This matters
even when it comes to the smallest details, such as, 'If I add one
more picture to my gallery wall will it throw off the balance?'
Think on it and give every decision the time it deserves.
Stay true to your story and don't fall into the trap of instant
gratification.

If you feel like an element is missing and you're struggling
to find special and meaningful pieces for your space, a trip to
an auction or craft fair can do wonders for the soul. You may
even find you're drawn to an item in a style that you love and
hadn't thought to use.

Time for Change?

Have you been living with your design and find you want to
make a change? If so, this needn't feel like a backward step.
Go back to your roadmap. Some elements may have changed
during your design process, but is the general story still there?
Does this new thing you love, or extra layer you want to add,
enhance the story or take it in a new fun direction? If so, great!
If not, why not? Have you outgrown your initial ideas or has
your story taken a dramatic new turn? This is a moment to
take stock and, luckily, since you know where you were
originally headed, you can use this to make a plan for how
to move forward.

PAGE 174

An imagined interior space designed
by Andrés Reisinger (see also page 179).

'Don't fixate
on the finish line.
Curate, don't
complete, and embrace
the evolution.'

Grass Roots

The rise of individualism has been well documented. We are encouraged to follow our dreams at all costs and to love ourselves. This book encourages you to listen to your own voice, but it is also key to widen your net of inspiration beyond yourself, refilling your creative pool with ideas that are outside of your comfort zone.

We need each other more than we think. As we have become increasingly isolated, connecting with others and creating a sense of community are more important than ever. New homes are becoming smaller, with spaces such as dining rooms disappearing as we choose to eat out or order takeaway. Lines are blurring as offices, bars, restaurants and even department stores offer a more home-like experience, encouraging you to treat their spaces like your own living room. Home is now wherever you lay your hat.

Take the tiny-house craze to its extreme and we see the rise in transformational furniture, such as beds that turn into sofas, or pull-out dining areas with tables and power built in to accommodate all your tech. The thought of millions of us spending our lives on a kind of platform for living, only interacting with the world through technology, is as scary as it is innovative.

Take time to reconnect with those around you. Bounce ideas off friends and family and visit others' homes to find inspiration. Think about how you will use your space with others. Is there anything you can try to create more togetherness in your home? Would switching things up in your dining area or living room create a more family-friendly space?

Colour unites this densely populated cityscape.

This rendered image by Andrés Reisinger imagines a future where homes are connected to nature and open to the world.

Chapter Eight

Authentic Sources
of Inspiration

Keep your home alive by seeking out new ideas
and design pieces that will benefit not just your space, but
also your lifestyle. From getting to know your local community
to getting in touch with nature, here are some things to think
about when it's time for a change in your interior.

Living Local

Making living lovely is about living authentically in the place you call home. Seek out local markets, new shop openings, vintage fairs and art-school shows in your area. Alongside meeting the makers and bringing a piece from your local area back home, you will also benefit your local economy and bring a moment of joy to the person from whom you buy your item.

Look, too, into the history of your local area. You may be down the road from where Josiah Wedgwood founded his world-class pottery or in a part of the world famous for its weaving. Dig a little to find new sources of inspiration and strengthen your feeling of belonging to the place where you live. Knowing what has been can help grow your confidence in where you are and help you identify where you want to go. Understanding the history of your home can set your creativity free.

Return to the Wild

As modern life has become increasingly complex and isolating, the natural reaction is to go back to nature, surrounding ourselves with things that connect us to plants, scenery and planet Earth. With the majority of the world's population living in cities, we may not all be able to escape to the countryside, but you can create your own wild oasis at home.

When we 'rewild' our homes, our planet also benefits. Return to sustainable materials and give mindful thought to how your things are made and their impact on the natural world. Sebastian Cox's designs in natural wood (left; see page 182) and the furniture of Tom Raffield (below) are great natural inspiration for us. Spend time in nature and investigate volunteering for local nature initiatives and charities. Helping out in nature can give a welcome respite from the intensity of digital life and also help unearth design ideas for your home.

'Creating not consuming, challenging not conforming, less stress, more happiness'

Sebastian and Brogan Cox

'We have created our home quite instinctively, using materials, tools and objects within our means'

This husband-and-wife team are forging a new design path that has its roots in nature and an eye on the future of our planet. Their passion for maintaining woodland is matched only by their drive for telling stories in the home, and their quality handmade furniture appears in stores and houses across the world. The story of their home has much to offer about living within our means, with creativity and feeling.

Our Interior Roadmap

Our three materials are wood, paper and wool. Our three colours are green, gold and white. The three feelings it evokes are togetherness, rejuvenation and ease, and its three key functions are creating, resting and socializing.

What Home Means to Us

We have created our home quite instinctively, using materials, tools and objects within our means. We haven't done this in pursuit of a particular scheme or aesthetic, yet our home has an accidental and rather wonderful cohesion, which comes from everything having a sense of meaning.

We live in a modern apartment in Southeast London with large windows looking out over the Thames, so it's very light and bright. We use our home as a canvas for the things we love. After viewing it, we discovered that Seb's ancestor worked as a waterman on our street and plied his trade on the river steps at the foot of our building.

The insides of our cupboards are lined with postcards and pictures, so every time we make a cup of tea or hunt for a tin of tomatoes, we can enjoy remembering the places we've been and things we've done. The challenge is creating enough space for everything. We have a cupboard of doom in the kitchen corner, full of candles, batteries, cables, Blu Tack and tins and we can't quite motivate ourselves to throw any of it away.

We don't own our home, so there's no escaping that it's temporary. Having a light footprint means we need to be creative in order to build a sense of homeliness and of 'us'.

Our most beloved thing at home is our dog, Willow! Our home hasn't been the same since she came along two years ago. Whenever either of us comes home to an empty apartment, we're reminded quite sharply of how precious she is and what a huge impact animals have on your home.

Relaxing and Entertaining

Lighting plays a critical role in creating relaxing spaces; we have lamps in every corner and I take great pleasure in candles. Spending time cooking and eating together is relaxing too; making a leisurely breakfast on a Saturday morning is a wonderful way to leave the working week behind. The music we listen to varies. If I'm baking, sewing or painting I'll listen to jazz, Talking Heads or Supertramp. If Seb has cooked dinner we might put Motown or northern soul on while we eat.

When it comes to dinner parties we love to have as many guests as we can fit. We move all the furniture, create one long table that spans our apartment and borrow our neighbours' oven space, crockery and cutlery! If our home were a movie it would be Wes Anderson's *Fantastic Mr Fox* (2009).

Chapter Eight

LEFT

Willow the dog in Seb and Brogan's
workshop in Deptford, London.

BELOW

The Sebastian Cox showroom.

OVERLEAF

A dreamy dining scene, hand-crafted
by the Sebastian Cox team.

GREEN	GOLD	WHITE
WOOD	PAPER	WOOL

The Evolving Home: It's Alive!

Chapter Eight

The Evolving Home: It's Alive!

The Future of Home

With AI art making waves, augmented reality changing the way we look at spaces and 3D-printed furniture becoming more and more accessible, how can you keep ahead of the curve? New isn't always better, so don't go chasing something just because it is the latest trend. The future is going to happen whatever we do and wondering about the next big thing shouldn't stop you from embracing the now. As with all things, balance is key.

ABOVE, LEFT

An imagined space designed by Carlos Neda with creative direction by Andrés Reisinger.

ABOVE, RIGHT

An imagined bedroom illustration by Charlotte Taylor, inspired by our Luca bed design (page 160).

Virtual Tools

Virtual interiors are huge on social media and lots of digital tools have been created to help you design your space. Rendered visualizations can't recreate the atmosphere and tactility that you experience in a real room, but they can be a useful part of the design process. This is an interesting progression in the interiors world and one that we must be aware of to understand how we live now and what the future of home might look like.

Perhaps because we are Xennials – stuck between the analogue and the digital ages – it's still important to us to sketch our designs using pencil and paper, as well as computer design tools. We enjoy first showing our clients real objects, surfaces and materials on a moodboard and then using digital illustrations to reinforce our designs and add specific details and lines to a space.

However you approach your designs, there is no denying that some of the most incredible spaces inspiring us on social media right now are rendered to perfection.

ABOVE

A curvy bedroom of dreams, designed by Andrés Reisinger.

Homes Illustrated

While new digital interior design tools are posing their own challenges and opportunities, digital and 3D-printed artwork is also on the rise and can be a wonderful way to enhance your space. The illustration opposite right is by digital artist Charlotte Taylor of our own home. Her artwork manages to straddle a wonderful middle ground between the analogue and the virtual worlds, depicting wonderful spaces with subtly textured combinations of colour and texture, simply assembled but somehow managing to convey atmosphere.

Dream House

The dream realities that can now be rendered in 3D and even virtual reality mean that our homes can be extensions of our imaginations. We are now in a time where we can choose to completely reinvent what home means to us. Virtual methods allow us to dream about designs that are not possible with current technology and materials, providing inspiration for new ways of thinking about our spaces and paving the way for new discoveries.

Harry Nuriev

'My home is my reality'

Harry Nuriev, New York-based Russian architect, artist and founder of Crosby Studios, is a wonder kid of the new design scene whose work is a breath of fresh air and full of futuristic vision. Prizing his wardrobe as his favourite part of his home, he has a no-holds-barred approach to colour and form that is inspired by fashion and has led to collaborations with Balenciaga, Nike and other major brands. We first saw his work at London Design Fair in a vast warehouse space that provided the perfect backdrop for Crosby Studios's strong statement pieces. His unique voice and the classical otherwordliness of his designs refused to be ignored.

My Interior Roadmap

The three materials that make a home for me are metal, vinyl and textile. My three colours are grey, hibiscus and jade, and the three feelings that say home to me are future, nostalgia and sexy. Three functions that are important to my life in my home are chilling, chilling, chilling.

What Home Means to Me

I live in an apartment in New York and my home is my reality – a mixture of memories and ideas about the future, with a good sense of humour. The environment I've created at home is crucial to me, it's my world, and the best part of it is my wardrobe.

Relaxing and Entertaining

My home is a private space for me and my family, but when I do entertain, four people is the ideal number for a dinner party. Unfortunately I find I'm rarely at home for longer than a week because I travel a lot, but when I do find time to relax at home, I like to do laundry, take a bath or simply do nothing. I listen to music by Kanye West, Kendrick Lamar or Travis Scott and if my home were a movie (I love this idea) it would be anything by Sofia Coppola.

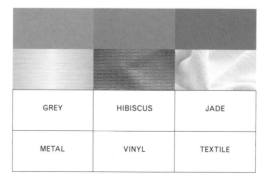

GREY	HIBISCUS	JADE
METAL	VINYL	TEXTILE

Harry's minimal colour-blocked kitchen in
his Brooklyn apartment has cool impact.

The Evolving Home: It's Alive!

Chapter Eight

A powerfully minimal dining space with a playful
central light made from blue ballpoint pens.

Hi there! View through the apartment with colour
drawing you in. Design by Crosby Studios.

The Evolving Home: It's Alive!

Before and After
...and After That

Your home will never be finished, nor should it be.
Don't be scared by this idea – embrace it and let it free you
from the panic of having a deadline. This is true of our home,
too. Here we show you how it has evolved, from being stripped
bare when we first bought it to all the looks we've
experimented with along the way.

The Hallway

When we first bought the house the hallway was painted
Pepto-Bismol pink, with green carpeted stairs (below), and
this bold colour scheme was honestly one of the things
that sold the house to us. We wanted to keep the pink, but
reinterpret it in our way, so we designed our own wallpaper
(right) to use in the space.

The Living Room

This room has gone through several incarnations since we
first bought the house (opposite, top), including a blue phase
specially created for a shoot to launch one of our print
collections (opposite, below left), but we always knew we
eventually wanted to reinstate the original wood panelling
and lay new floors (opposite, below right).

A Note on Grit

Any creative endeavour can stretch you to the limit, but that means you are right where you should be. Endless decisions, financial blows, unavoidable changes and mistakes are all part of the design journey you mapped out from the start. Nothing comes easy, so don't expect to be able to create something life-changing and meaningful without effort, heart and grit.

Of these three, grit really is the key. We all have an inner creativity and ideas come and go, but the real difference between making living lovely and not, is your determination to deliver. When that last bit of woodchip is threatening to finish you, hang on in there. When you are doubting if you will ever be able to get through the mess and dust, remember: you can do it. There is nothing more rewarding than making something for yourself and seeing it benefit your life, and there is nothing more powerful than grit.

The Evolving Home: It's Alive!

Our Roadmap

The final home story in this book is our own. We want to show you how we used our tools to guide us from first ideas right through to our home as it looks today.

Three Colours

The three colours that we chose for our home were pink, Yves Klein blue and malachite green.

Three Functions

The three key functions our home had to fulfil were to be relaxing, inspiring and a great party space.

Three Feelings

The three feelings we wanted our home to evoke were safe, unique and comfortable.

Three Materials

Our three materials are washed oak, velvet and matt and gloss tiles.

Home Title

The Joyful Minimalist Home

Perry Rise, London

Our Victorian detached house in Southeast London is our live–work space and passion project. Its design is inspired by found objects and prints from within the house as well as our own travels. The house's previous owners clearly also had a passion for interiors: they had pink walls and deep-green carpets throughout and left a stash of old interior magazines and fabric swatches from the 1950s and 60s in the loft.

As the house has evolved with us, it has gone through many stages, acting both as a home and as a backdrop for our work as designers. So far we have restored the roof, the original sash windows and the floors. We have completed the pink bathroom, updated the front door, given ourselves a 'wonder closet' WC and created an entrance hallway the previous owners would have loved (we hope!). The open-plan kitchen–diner–studio space is the heart of the project and has inspired many of our product designs.

Our garden's central apple tree, old English roses and camellia tree have had a major impact on our designs for the interior – inspiring our colour palette and floral motifs.

LEFT

The graphic wallpaper in our hallway is called
Felt Tip, and was hand-drawn as part of our wallpaper
collection for Graham & Brown. The stair carpet was
based on an archive period carpet from 1870,
the year the house was built.

BELOW AND OPPOSITE

We designed this sofa (below) as part of a
collection for Love Your Home and called it Tilda after
our favourite actor, Tilda Swinton. The curved back is
handmade in Britain. The Luca bed, as seen in our
bedrooms (opposite and page 160), is also part of the
collecton and is named after our favourite
director, Luca Guadagnino.

Chapter Eight

Open Mind = Open Home

An open home will have unfinished bits – the odd chip in the paintwork, a stain you couldn't get out, a room you haven't quite got right, a paint colour that doesn't make you smile yet, a cushion too many and a plant too few. An open home lets your friends in to spill red wine on your new worktop and embraces the marks on the floorboards that come with life (and high heels). An open home is somewhere that your family gather and your friends come to when they get dumped on. It is a space to make new friends and start new ideas that could take your life in unexpected directions.

The journey of designing your home is about the experience of living in your space and evolving with it, and the only destination is happiness. This might sound cheesy, but there is a beauty in every stage of your design journey, whether you are building your own house, styling a shelving unit in your first pad or decorating your childhood bedroom. The point is, it is not a race and no part of that journey is more or less valid than another.

Our 'Insta-famous' pink bathroom – one of the first spaces we designed and installed – is a haven of simple materiality and colour, with its curvy forms and heritage hardware.

Welcoming guests into our spare bedroom with colour and pattern.

Openness is everything. Be open to learning from others, open to your own creative journey and open to inviting joy in. Even the most experienced interior designer has much to learn from new and exciting designers on the scene, just as a child can learn from their design-savvy uncle (we are looking at you, Phoebe, Lara, Freya, Seren, Jasper, Austin, Zac, Freddie, Gene and Wilbur).

One person's soulless white box is another's sleek minimalist dream. Create a space that is right for you and fill it with the ideas and stories that make you feel good. There is no special secret here and no perfect recipe. If it feels right then run to it, play with it and fight for it. Design for yourself and your home will be true and thrillingly so. If you can learn to crystallize your personal style, you will not only be leagues ahead of those around you, but you will have designed a home that makes life better for you and everyone around you.

Chapter Eight

The shoe storage dream was a top priority
for our renovation, with signature arched wardrobes and
squiggle detailing on the cabinetry, a motif that
occurs through our house.

Our serene kitchen space for relaxing and entertaining.
Form and texture bring the simple palette to life.

One of our favourite places to be, whether working
on the main table or entertaining friends and family.
This table really is the heart of our home.

The Evolving Home: It's Alive!

2LG Sourcebook

Here's a cheeky list of our favourite suppliers and designers to give you a head start on your pad.

Movies to Watch

2001: A Space Odyssey (1968)
Batman Returns (1992)
Big (1988)
Blade Runner (1982)
Blade Runner 2049 (2017)
I Am Love (2009)
Labyrinth (1986)
McQueen (2018)
Prospero's Books (1991)
Roma (2018)
Sex and the City (1998–2010)
Suspiria (1977)
Stoker (2013)
The Favourite (2018)
The Grand Budapest Hotel (2014)

Playlist

Christine and the Queens
For when you need to remember that boxes don't exist

Dear Evan Hansen
For your inner musical theatre geek

Lisa Ekdahl, *When Did You Leave Heaven?*
For when you are feeling the love

Florence and the Machine
For your inner goddess – we all have one

Philip Glass, *The Hours*
For meditative moments

Keith Jarrett, *The Köln Concert*
For mind expansion

Annie Lennox
For nostalgia

Little Mix
For strutting

London Grammar
For the soul

Michael Nyman
For your creative mind

Arvo Pärt
For ultimate inner moments

Radiohead
For the tortured moments we all endure

RuPaul, 'Sissy That Walk'
For when you feel so real

Places to Visit

Acne Studios, Worldwide
www.acnestudios.com

Aesop Stores, Worldwide
www.aesop.com

Barbican Centre, London
Silk St,
London EC2Y 8DS,
United Kingdom
www.barbican.org.uk

Broadway, New York
Broadway,
Manhattan, New York,
USA

Color Factory, New York
251 Spring St,
New York, NY 10013,
USA
www.colorfactory.co

Design Museum, London
224–238 Kensington High St,
London W8 6AG,
United Kingdom
www.designmuseum.org

HAY House, Copenhagen
Østergade 61, 2,
1100 København,
Denmark
www.hay.dk

Hotel Saint-Marc, Paris
36 Rue Saint-Marc,
75002 Paris,
France
www.hotelsaintmarc.com

sketch, London
9 Conduit St, Mayfair,
London W1S 2XG,
United Kingdom
www.sketch.london

Liberty, London
Regent St,
London W1B 5AH,
United Kingdom
www.libertylondon.com

La Muralla Roja, Calpe
Partida Manzanera, 3,
03710 Calpe, Alicante,
Spain

National Theatre, London
Upper Ground,
Lambeth, London SE1 9PX,
United Kingdom
www.nationaltheatre.org.uk

Royal Academy of Arts, London
Burlington House, Piccadilly,
London W1J 0BD,
United Kingdom
www.rca.ac.uk

Victoria and Albert Museum, London
Cromwell Rd, Knightsbridge,
London SW7 2RL,
United Kingdom
www.vam.ac.uk

Villa Necchi Campiglio, Milan
Via Mozart, 14,
20122 Milano MI,
Italy
www.casemuseo.it

Where to Buy

1882 Ltd
Stunning pottery with some amazing
collaborations from Paul Smith
to Peter Pilotto.
1882ltd.com

&tradition
Furniture, lighting and accessories,
with clean lines, subtle colours and a
beautiful use of materials.
www.andtradition.com

Anthropologie
For pieces with a global feel that
are beautifully curated, with a strong
craft vibe.
www.anthropologie.com

BISQUE
Stunning coloured radiators –
if you have to have them, make 'em
look good!
www.bisque.co.uk

Bitossi
Their Rimini blue collection is instantly
recognizable. but they also have a huge
range of other beautiful ceramic pieces.
www.bitossihome.it

Caesarstone
For great composite worktops.
www.caesarstone.co.uk

Calico Wallpaper
The BEST print designers in all of NYC,
and a gorgeous couple to boot.
www.calicowallpaper.com

Cameron Design House
Stunning lighting all made to order.
www.camerondesignhouse.com

Clarke & Clarke
For fabric by the metre – we
use them a lot for plain material
and basic linens and velvets.
clarke-clarke.com

COS
Worn by every designer
and architect, always.
www.cosstores.com

C. P. Hart
A great bathroom supplier, they have all
the best brands in one place and plenty
of helpful knowledge, too.
www.cphart.co.uk

Crown Paints
Fun and playful trend-led paint company.
www.crownpaints.co.uk

CUSTHOM
London-based print studio and
collaborators of ours, Kylie Jenner has
one of their prints in her dining room.
www.custhom.co.uk

Decode
Great contemporary lighting.
Their designs by Dan Schofield
are favourites of ours.
www.decode.london

Denby Pottery
One of the UK's oldest producers of
pottery, classic and beautifully crafted.
www.denbypottery.com

eBay
We use eBay a lot for vintage
furniture. It's a great place to find things
to be reupholstered.
www.ebay.com

Ercol
Great classic British furniture,
handmade with a retro vibe.
www.ercol.com

Farrow & Ball
Classic, timeless paints – one of
the best names around.
www.farrow-ball.com

Floor Story
Rugs for every occasion,
with some amazing designer
collaborations (including us!).
floorstory.co.uk

Graham & Brown
Wallpaper for every taste at a great
price range.
www.grahambrown.com

GUBI
Danish glamour, with simple
shapes and luxurious finishes.
www.gubi.com

Havwoods
Our go-to engineered-wood
flooring supplier.
www.havwoods.com

HAY
Danish design at its BEST,
from furniture to accessories –
fun and minimal.
hay.dk

IKEA
Always great, always affordable.
www.ikea.com

James Shaw
Leading the way with recycled plastic, James makes Baroque pieces that are the design classics of the future.
jamesmichaelshaw.co.uk

John Lewis of Hungerford
Handmade kitchens, with great craftsmanship and a myriad of options available.
www.john-lewis.co.uk

Johnson Tiles
For a wonderful range of colours, shapes and finishes. We use their basic square tiles in matt and gloss a lot!
www.johnson-tiles.com

Jonathan Adler
Always fun, and always colourful, we have had a long-standing love affair with JA.
uk.jonathanadler.com

Kast Concrete Basins
Fancy a colourful concrete bathroom basin? These are our go-to.
kastconcretebasins.com

Kvadrat
Real leaders in textiles. Raf Simons has been a long-time collaborator of the brand and his collections are always stunning!
kvadrat.dk

Ligne Roset
French design, with added style.
www.ligne-roset.com

Love Your Home
Sofas and beds, handmade in England.
www.love-your-home.co.uk

MADE
Design-led pieces at high-street prices.
www.made.com

MENU
Stunningly simple shapes and fine-lined furniture, based in Copenhagen.
www.menu.as

mind the cork
Sustainable home accessories, with style.
www.mindthecork.co.uk

Mylands Paint
A heritage paint company who are great for bold colour and saturation.
www.mylands.com

Nest
An amazing online shop with a mid century heart, they stock all the classic furniture brands and are a great resource.
www.nest.co.uk

Normann Copenhagen
This really fun and colourful brand are our go-to for a modern Scandi look.
www.normann-copenhagen.com

NOVOCASTRIAN
With a northern heart and soul, this small artisan company in the UK make metalwork into stunning furniture.
novocastrian.co

Olivia Aspinall Studio
Surface design, making terrazzo fun, modern and colourful.
www.olivia-aspinall.com

Piñatex
A leather alternative made from pineapple.
www.ananas-anam.com

Pinch Design
London-made stunningly detailed furniture that is simple and timeless. Think British craft heirloom pieces.
pinchdesign.com

Pulpo
Glam, futuristic homeware, with a dark and fun 'space' aesthetic.
pulpoproducts.com

Sebastian Cox
A true woodsman, Cox makes stunning furniture – future heirlooms.
www.sebastiancox.co.uk

Sight Unseen
Online Interiors porn, beautifully curated, super-cutting edge and inspiring in the extreme.
www.sightunseen.com

Smile Plastics
Makers of recycled-plastic surfaces – we've made tables and vanity with their materials, which always gets plenty of attention!
www.smile-plastics.com

Super Mundane
An artist we love for bold graphic impact. If you like colour you will love this.
supermundane.com

Surface View
Murals for every design style, from Victoria and Albert Museum prints to the first man on the moon.
www.surfaceview.co.uk

Swedish Ninja
A super playful homeware brand, as the name suggests!
www.swedishninja.com

Tom Dixon
Always bold and innovative and has great lighting at different scales.
www.tomdixon.net

Vinterior
An online shop for everything vintage, from art to furniture.
www.vinterior.com

west elm
If you like mid century modern, you will love west elm.
www.westelm.co.uk

Yuta Segawa
A ceramic artist specializing in minatures – a collector's dream.
www.yutasegawa.com

Zip Hydrotap
This tap will change your life – you're welcome!
www.zipwater.co.uk

Acknowledgments
and Credits

About the Authors

Russell Whitehead has always been a writer at heart, with a love of words and telling stories. He studied English Literature at Warwick University, then trained professionally as an actor and singer at the Royal Academy of Music, London. His inquisitive mind has always kept his creativity active and even as he spent many years performing in London's West End, the designs of the sets, costumes and theatres themselves were fascinating to him. His personal growth led him to develop his skills as a designer and meeting his husband, Jordan, was the catalyst that made this big career change happen. He believes in the idea that we are all many things. We don't need to fit into boxes and creativity can cross any boundary.

Jordan Cluroe was born and raised in the West Midlands, UK, and has had a love for design, particularly fashion, from an early age. His confident character has always led him to unexpected places in his career and he enjoys spreading that confidence and empowering people to be the best versions of themselves. He trained originally at the Liverpool Institute of Performing Arts and worked in televison and theatre in London before finding his true passion in design. As co-founder of 2LG Studio with his husband, Russell, he is passionate about a creative way of life for all and both love to write for their blog and for their weekly design column in London's Metro newspaper.

Acknowledgments

To the dashing Dan Hopwood, thank you for taking us under your wing. We will always remember our long chats high up in our design digs in Milan. To the lovely Sophie Robinson, for championing our use of colour, especially that pink rocking chair. And Tom Dyckoff for being such a lovely gent and sharing your architectural passion with us. Thank you to Nick Canham, Aoife Rice and our incredible editors at the *Metro* and *Gay Times* for helping us to grow. To our small group of incredible friends (you know who you are) for your words of wisdom that kept us on track and continue to do so. Thank you to the most open and encouraging of journalists, Kat Burroughs and Claudia Bailie, your support has meant the world to us. To the glorious Robert Hasty for your foresight and for giving us an incredible opportunity with Ligne Roset at the beginning of our journey as designers. To Toni and the team at Nest.co.uk for your passion and bravery in doing it your own way and allowing us to be a part of that. To Alan at Graham & Brown and Yvonne at Brintons for letting us into their archives, and to Kiran and Rebecca and Jess at John Lewis of Hungerford for being so up for it and having the bravery to follow through. To all of our design collaborators for your charm and creativity. To our lovely clients for allowing us on their journey with them and for being brave enough to let us take them in new directions. And to Megan for being there with us all the way, making each shoot much more lovely. To all of our followers, you keep us inspired and buoyed up with your passion about your homes and the world of design. You have been so loyal and your positivity keeps us going. To all those brave designers and makers and content creators on social media who have enriched our lives, we consider ourselves so honoured to call you friends and to be a part of this brave new digital world with you. Hold onto your creativity, never let hate or doubt or jealousy take hold and try to focus on your love for what you do and for those around you. Kindness is the way forward and we can all come up together if we learn from one another. Don't fear the unknown and trust in positivity.

Picture Credits

All photography is by Megan Taylor unless otherwise noted below.

T=top, B=bottom, L=left, R=right, C=centre.

Acne Studios: 39BC, 158TR, 159BR; **Aesop, photo by Paola Pansini, interior design by Dimore Studio:** 39TC; **Alamy Stock Photo:** Zoonar GmbH: 56TC; Andreas von Einsiedel: 57TL; Chris Hellier: 57TC; **Alun Callender:** 57BC, 159C, 180L, 183B, 183L, 184–185; **Jordan Cluroe:** 161BR; **Cogolin:** 171B; **Paul Craig:** 168–169; **Jake Curtis:** 160; **Design by 2LG Studio for Crown Paints, photo by Max Attenborough:** 82L, 82R, 162L; **Dimore Studio at Hotel Saint Marc:** 91T, 91BR, 158C; **Edition Van Treeck:** 77; **Olafur Eliasson:** 38R: *Your uncertain shadow* (2010) by Olafur Eliasson, photo: María del Pilar García Ayensa/Studio Olafur Eliasson, © 2010 Olafur Eliasson; **Andrea Ferrari:** 92–93; **Federico Floriani:** 87; **Joe Gamble:** 12; **Gubi:** 76;

Nick Hudson: 31BR, 32–33; **Jay's Photo/ Getty Images:** 31BLC, 75BLR and 91BLL; **Ingmar Kerth:** 56TR; **Dirk Vander Kooij:** 111TL, 111BR; **Mikhail Loskutov:** 189–191; **Mattia Lotti:** 172 173; **Mud Australia:** 131T; **Pulpo:** 75T, 75BR; **Tom Raffield:** 180R; **Andrés Reisinger:** 174, 179, 186L, 187; **Shutterstock:** Chingraph: 31BLL, 47BLL, 75BLL, 131BLL and 188L; Heiko Kueverling: 31BLR; *Batman Returns* (1992), Warner Bros/DC Comics/ Kobal: 38L; Willy Barton: 39TL; Everett Collection: 39BR; optimarc: 47BLC, 170R and 183BLL; Freedom-Photo: 47BLR; J. Lekavicius: 57BL; Adam Scull/Photolink.Net/Mediapunch: 58T; dubassy: 58B; Purple Moon: 75BLC; Magdalena Cvetkovic: 91BLC; Aligusak: 91BLR; Turica: 106R; Rodin Anton: 111TRL; Ye.Maltsev: 111TRC; Billion Photos: 111TRR; *Labyrinth* (1986), Jim Henson Productions/Kobal: 126L; SosnaRadosna: 131BLC; IBL: 158L; Tinxi: 159BL; Chinnapong: 170C; Sunflowery: 178; YamabikaY: 183BLC;

Kira Volkov: 183BLR; pedphoto36pm: 188C; Patty Chan: 188R; **Silica stone by Alusid, image by Tom Ainsworth:** 108R; **Smile Plastics:** 18TR, 104; **Studio 65, Bocca sofa, 1970. Courtesy of Gufram:** 166; **Kris Tamburello:** 48–49; **Charlotte Taylor:** 186R; **Petrina Tinslay:** 131R; **Wallpaper design by 2LG Studio for Graham & Brown:** 14 ('Felt Tip'), 18L ('Labyrinth'); **Natalie Weiss:** 170L, 171TR; **Mami Yamada:** 47T; **Manolo Yllera:** 31T; **Tim Young:** 84–85

Index

Page numbers in *italics* refer to illustrations